"This book is thoug[...]
of wisdom and pra[...]
considering adoption or have already adopted but also for birth
parents and for parents in blended families. Many who read
this book will find practical applications for immediate needs,
and all who read it will be blessed, as was I." —Tom

"This is a beautiful book! It is so gripping. I had no trouble
reading straight through it. I cried tears of joy, got goose-bumps,
laughed, and found myself praying for you again as you continue
your journey." —Teresa

"This book is informational, educational, encouraging and
interesting to read all at once." —Heather

"What a significant contribution this book will make to the
lives of many families." —Elaine

"I will say that I cried when I read some of the parts about Jade's
tummy mommy letters. The tears were just flowing. This book
reminds me of 2 Corinthians 1:3-4 where we are told to comfort
others with the comfort we receive from God." —Kathryn

"This book is entirely wonderful! The content is thorough, giving
people in the waiting lounges of adoption wise advice when
planning for the long haul, both practically and emotionally.
I especially appreciate your honesty on realistic bonding with
older children: it's rarely instantaneous, and often more of
a choice to love versus waiting for a feeling to love (which is
also true when parenting older biological children, as you well
know)." —Kelly

"You wouldn't think that a book on adoption would be a page-
turner, but I found myself wanting to know what happened
next after each chapter." —Mary

Nine Year Pregnancy

*Waiting on God–Our Journey
of Adoption*

Delana H. Stewart

CROSSBOOKS
PUBLISHING

CrossBooks™
A Division of LifeWay
1663 Liberty Drive
Bloomington, IN 47403
www.crossbooks.com
Phone: 1-866-879-0502

First published by CrossBooks 12/27/2011

ISBN: 978-1-4627-1305-9 (sc)
ISBN: 978-1-4627-1306-6 (e)

Scripture quotations marked (CEV) are taken from the Contemporary English
Version® Copyright © 1995 American Bible Society. All rights reserved.

Scripture quotations marked (KJV) are taken from the King James Version and are in
the public domain.

Scripture quotations marked (ISV) are taken from the Holy Bible: International
Standard Version®. Copyright © 1996-2008 by the ISV Foundation. ALL RIGHTS
RESERVED INTERNATIONALLY. Used by permission.

Scripture quotations marked (NASB) are taken from the New American Standard
Bible®, Copyright © 1960, 1962, 1963, 1968, 1971, 1972, 1973, 1975, 1977, 1995
by The Lockman Foundation. Used by permission. (www.Lockman.org)

Scripture quotations marked (NIV) are taken from the Holy Bible, New International
Version®, NIV®. Copyright © 1973, 1978, 1984, 2011 by Biblica, Inc.™ Used by
permission of Zondervan. All rights reserved worldwide. www.zondervan.com.
The "NIV" and "New International Version" are trademarks registered in the
United States Patent and Trademark Office by Biblica, Inc.™ NLT—New Living
Translation, 2007, Tyndale House Publishers.

Printed in the United States of America

Birthday photo and toy store photo by family friend Mary Watts Clutts. Arabian Gulf
photo and family portrait by family friend Stephen Draper. All other photos taken by
James Stewart and family.

For Jade, our little princess

Contents

Foreword

Adoption . . . you can't get much closer to the heart of God. Over and over, we see throughout scripture His command for us to take care of orphans. God placed this command on Delana Stewart's heart many years ago. She clearly heard the call of adoption ring right out to her family. This was God's will for them, but how many of us now realize that following God's will for your life isn't always the easy path?

Closed doors, missed appointments, being moved around to different parts of the world definitely made the road to their adoption a bumpy one, but none the less, it was the road God wanted them to travel. It's so easy to lose heart, hope and faith in God when we can't see the big picture. HE always sees the big picture, and He is teaching us all to be more like Him as we face the challenges and joys that He places in our lives.

In *Nine Year Pregnancy* Delana shares her story openly and honestly. Private journal prayers, poems and songs, tug on your heart as you yearn along with her for a precious orphan to be placed into her loving home. Along with sharing the journey that leads up to their adoption, Delana beautifully captures the moment of meeting their daughter, Jade. Her genuine compassion for the child that God created for her family shines brightly through this section of the story. Transparently discussing the frustrations, fears and raw emotions that adoptive families face in the first few years are helpful and so needed. Families who face the same road will be encouraged by the consistency of the Stewart family as they pour love on their daughter and sister.

Yes, adoption is near to the heart of God. Throughout the pages of this book, you will find a family who is also near to God's heart. I recommend this book to anyone who has adopted or is praying about adopting. While this story is about the adoption journey, it also serves as a wonderful encouragement to anyone who needs that extra bit of hope in knowing that God hears their prayers and that His timing is always perfect.

Renee Crosse
Visit Renee and her husband Clay at --
http://www.holyhomes.org

Preface

OMINOUS CLOUDS BLOCKED all light from the moon. Lightning lit up the sky and thunder boomed almost instantly—another Texas thunderstorm. The black night darkened when flickering street lights went out. The wipers swished back and forth furiously while horizontal rain pounded the windshield of our '89 Pontiac Parisienne. The howling winds drowned out the radio, as our car inched on down the winding road. Suddenly, something appeared in the road ahead of us. The car screeched to a halt when my husband slammed on the brakes. I noticed in the glow of the headlights a little girl drenched by the downpour. Jumping out of the car, I quickly approached the girl saying, "Hi Sweetie, where is your mommy?"

"Mommy's gone . . ." she whimpered, tears mingling with the falling rain.

My heart raced. I tried to figure out what was happening. Had there been an accident? Broken glass littered the road but no car. Who is this girl? Where are her parents? Why is she standing out here in the rain? I wrapped my arms around her trying to comfort her. A fierce need to love, protect and care for this child overwhelmed me. Where am I? When will this torrential rain storm cease? What do I do?

"Take this child. Take care of her. She is for you. I place the lonely in families," a deep voice responded.

Suddenly I woke up in our bed breathing fast, heart still pounding, while my husband James slept quietly beside me. Was it only a dream? It was so vivid, so real! I recognized the words spoken by the deep voice, God's voice. I could not get back to sleep because of a strong feeling that a little girl somewhere needed me. I tiptoed down the hall to check on our three sons, aged two, four and six, who slept peacefully in a nearby room. I kissed each one gently on his forehead and quietly returned to my room. Sliding back into bed, I wondered, "Do I dare tell my husband that I think perhaps we need to adopt a little girl when we have three sons who need our love, support, attention and time?" Nah! It was only a dream.

Yet this dream would shake up our world. This dream would take me from being contented with family life, church, worldview and relationships to breathtaking heights and deep, painful valleys. Does God still speak through dreams? Would I have faith for the journey ahead, no matter how long or difficult the path, or would I be dashed to pieces on the jagged rocks of the canyon?

Acknowledgements

I am very grateful to God for bringing our family on this journey and giving me the ability to express my thoughts in this way. This book would not have been written without the love, encouragement and patience of my husband James and our daughter Jade. I also wish to thank Kathryn, not only for her helpful insights, but also for saying with her sweet Southern accent, "Delana, you really should write a book and tell your story."

Many others have also made this book a reality. I want to thank our sons and daughter-in-law—Jordan, Jacob, Joshua and Juliana—for helping me choose the title and for giving me much needed feedback. Thank you, Stephen, for offering plot development ideas. Many friends and family members edited this manuscript: Patti and Tom (my parents), James, Mary, Teresa, Kathryn, Elaine, Kelly, Mandy and Heather. I especially appreciate my mom and the attention to detail that she gave in her countless hours of editing this book (she only thought she had retired from editing). Thank you all for your help, love, friendship and encouragement. Thanks to my many friends who prayed us through the decade-long adoption journey: Beth, Machelle, Teresa, Elaine, Karma, Allen, Chris, Janet, Bonnie, Jonathan, Shelly, Kathy, Cheryl, Darlene, Connie, Linda, Dan, Eileen, Karla, Ammy, Sally, Jane Ellen, Sarah and so many more!

Thanks to my twin-sister Deanna, her husband Randy and his relatives for prayer and guidance during our final stages of adoption. I also want to thank my parents, in-laws, siblings, other relatives and church family for welcoming Jade into our family.

Finally, a very special thank you to my husband James for the cover photos and the wonderful way he captured this book about our journey.

1. Conception

"And they lived happily ever after."

Many young newlyweds enter married life with this dreamy phrase firmly brain-washed into their minds. Many single women and men deeply desire to find that one special person with whom to share their lives—their joys and sorrows, their 2.5 children, one dog, one cat, two car garage—and then grow old and crinkly together. Some spend years wondering when their handsome prince or beautiful princess will waltz into their lives and choose them. Some married couples try year after year to have at least one of those 2.5 children, and yet they remain barren. But that's not *my* story.

Along with many others in my 1987 graduating class, I pursued a higher education, leaving behind the beauty and culture of San Antonio and heading off to a university in a tiny town in central Texas. Unlike other graduates, however, I did not dream about a lucrative career and a prestigious degree. I desired more than anything to be a godly wife and mother. Obtaining a degree in elementary education made the most sense because of my desire to someday have children of my own. By the beginning of my second semester, my knight in shining armor found me (an ordinary girl, from an ordinary family). James and I got to know each other in the campus cafeteria where we joined our roommates and suitemates who often ate meals together.

One day during lunch, I shared with this group of friends a difficult trial I was going through—getting out of an abusive relationship. Afterwards, James suggested that

1

the following weekend I accompany him to a local nursing home he frequently visited. He said that listening to others' burdens and caring for their needs would take my mind off my own troubles. We also spent time together attending concerts and movies on campus, studying at local diners and playing Frisbee. By springtime, when trees and flowers bloomed all over campus, he was contemplating whether or not he wanted to spend the rest of his life with me.

"Delana," he asked one day after we had spent the afternoon playing Frisbee in a nearby park, "if you were unable to have children, would you want to adopt?"

I did not need to ponder this question at all. Having a deep longing in my soul, and knowing that a strong desire to be a mother existed within my heart, I immediately exclaimed, "Yes, absolutely!"

Every afternoon, I participated in a program called Latch Key for underprivileged children. During this time I would spend time helping children with homework, playing with them and mentoring them when they got out of school. I could not imagine being only a wife and not also a mother.

On another day, when the sorrow of past hurts weighed heavily in my soul, James had me stand just outside the campus chapel, one of many red brick buildings that lined the university's main road. He asked me to tell him what I saw.

"School buildings, walls, the chapel, that's about it," I replied.

Then, James drove me out to a high place that overlooked the whole town, and he pointed out the campus chapel spire in the distance and asked again, "Now what do you see?"

"I see everything! I see all the campus buildings, all the houses, all the shops." That vantage point offered an amazing view of the tiny town in which we lived. I could even hear the chapel bells resounding in the distance.

James told me that I had been viewing life's challenges from the perspective I had down among the campus buildings, closed in, limited, small; but God saw every single detail. God's perspective of my situation was like the viewpoint we had up at the scenic overlook. He encouraged me to trust God with my problems and concerns. During the fifteen-minute drive back to the campus, he inquired, "Have you ever thought about living overseas?"

Actually, on many occasions throughout my childhood I wondered what it would be like to live in another country, learn another language, try new foods and meet new people. When I was growing up, my dad served in the Air Force and often went on trips to interesting places like Thailand, the Philippines and Korea; he always brought back exciting souvenirs for my siblings and me. As a teenager, I had been invited to speak on a panel of students discussing religions around the world. Was I interested in experiencing another country first hand? Yes, indeed!

Discussions about family life, cultures abroad and viewpoints on Scripture filled hours of conversation while James and I got to know one another better over the course of several months. On Mother's Day, he took me back to that scenic overlook of our little college town and asked me to marry him. Proposing at that very place was like saying: "God sees the big picture, and I believe you and I are in that picture together." Three months later, August 13, 1988, before the start of our fall semester, we stood in my parents' church before our family and friends and vowed to stay married through sickness and health—to death.

In 1989, James graduated, and we left our sleepy college town—he with a BA, and I with an *MRS* (I would finish my education degree 20 years later). Before settling down, we traveled to New Mexico, Colorado and Wyoming learning about different cultures within the U.S. and about ourselves. The 2.5 children were not long in coming. Our first two sons came sixteen months apart in September 1990 and January 1992.

The announcement of our first pregnancy occurred in Wyoming, where we cut our travel plans short and returned to Texas to settle in the Dallas/Ft. Worth Metro-plex to work and continue schooling. James was laid off after the birth of our second son, so we moved to Austin where he found work with a major computer company and then a software group. I stayed at home and took care of the boys, using my passion for education even in their early years.

Because of medical problems with my second pregnancy, the doctors advised me not to have any more children; so, we tried not to get pregnant for awhile. With two small children around all the time, we found ourselves in desperate need of a break. Grandparents lived nearby and gladly volunteered to watch the children so we could take a weekend getaway. We stayed in a condo on the beach, and we enjoyed the time we were able to invest in one another and in our marriage. Nine months later, February 1994, we had our third child.

"Honey," I told James after the ultrasound had undeniably revealed another boy, "that's what happens when you ask God for a quiver full of sons." Following a very difficult delivery, the doctor advised us not to have any more children, so I had a tubal ligation. No matter. By age 25 all my childhood dreams had come true: God blessed me with a wonderful husband and three healthy, beautiful sons!

Shortly after our third son came along, we bought our first home—a fixer-upper. While living there about two years, we fixed it up and sold it for a profit. Early in 1996, we invested those funds in the "perfect" house on an acre of land out in the countryside south of Austin. I remember the first time we stepped out of our car to look at that white stone house with blue-gray trim. We had always lived in congested cities or towns near traffic or train tracks or other noises. In the country it was so quiet we could hear a cow mooing in the distance. Our street housed twenty-five one-acre lots that ended in a cul-de-sac. All the lots backed up to farm and ranch land. What would have normally been acceptable outside voices for three boys suddenly sounded extremely loud. I shushed them so I could drink in the peacefulness of country living. I knew that once we moved in, I would have to let the boys use their outside voices in the great outdoors, but the day we visited I needed serenity. On move-in day James and I agreed, "We could live here for twenty years!"

Before our sons were born, we had pursued living overseas, but it did not work out at that time. The idea eventually faded from our minds. With a house full of little feet, it no longer appeared we would need to adopt. God had answered our prayers for family and a home.

Life was good. We were content. Content, that is, until the dream.

I do not remember anything particular about the week leading up to that life-changing dream. James worked 9-6, Monday through Friday, thirty minutes from home in a nearby city as a computer network administrator. I kept the house, cooked wholesome meals and taught our sons to read and write. On Saturdays, James could be seen on the riding lawn mower or tending our garden (with three little helpers in tow). On Sundays, we attended a small country church where we heavily involved ourselves with children and youth ministries.

It was a hot August evening in 1996. I likely put the boys to bed by 8:30 p.m. and either watched TV with James or read a novel. By 9:30 or 10:00 p.m., I probably crawled into bed, for I tend to be the early-to-bed type. Was it a Sunday night? Perhaps. Or, Monday.

" . . . Where am I? When will this torrential rain storm cease? What do I do?"

"Take this child. Take care of her. She is for you. I place the lonely in families," a deep voice responded.

Suddenly I woke up in our bed. It was only a dream.

A few days later, I took our boys for their weekly trip to the public library for story time. The Story Lady enchanted them once again with a delightful story about pancakes, which she followed up by letting each of the children help her make pancakes in an electric skillet in the craft room. Before leaving the library, our four-year-old son with sticky little maple-syrup fingers handed me a printed bookmark that read: 1-800-ADOPT-A-CHILD. Then, on the drive home, our oldest son commented on the big billboard with the picture of a child on it, which also read 1-800-ADOPT-A-CHILD. Was this more than a road sign? Nah! Just a coincidence.

The first week passed slowly; I daily felt burdened by the dream. "Do I talk to my husband about it?" my mind wondered repeatedly throughout the week. "What if he thinks I'm crazy? Am I crazy? How could this dream have been any more than just a strange dream?" Several times I started to tell James, but then I lost my nerve.

The weekend came, accompanied by a sinus infection and headache. My husband drove the boys to our little country church Sunday night without me. As I lay on my bed calling out to God to either lift the burden I felt from the dream or give me direction in whether or not to discuss it with my husband, the phone rang.

"Hello?" I answered after clearing the frog in my throat.

"Hi, this is Liz. I used to be your neighbor, remember me?"

"Of course," I said, recalling how her only son and my oldest son used to play together in the backyard in the city where we had bought our first home.

"I found my birth mother!" Liz exclaimed, continuing to tell me a long story about finding her birth mother when she had not even been looking for her.

Amazed, since I did not know she had even been adopted as a child, a tear slid down my cheek. By the end of the hour-long phone call we both were crying when she said, "I don't know why I felt such a pressing need to call and tell you this."

With tear-filled eyes my crackly voice replied, "I . . . I know why . . ."

I hung up the phone and knew with certainty that the minute my husband got home from church I needed to tell him about the dream. The dream that would change our lives forever . . .

2. Expecting

"Where there is no vision, the people perish . . ."
(Proverbs 29:18a KJV).

In our ranch-style house, the kitchen and dining area faced the backyard and cow pasture. During the phone call with Liz, I had been sitting at our dining table staring out the sliding glass door. I walked over into our galley-style kitchen to get something to drink and sat back down. The sun began to set over the pastureland behind our house, while I sat at our table sipping the hot, orange-spiced tea (my mother's recipe and "cure" for the common cold, flu and sinus infections).

Some amount of time had passed, with me deep in thought from Liz's phone call. The car rolled up the driveway and into the detached garage. Each of the boys came in quietly and gave me a hug. My oldest son, Josh, asked me if I felt better. "Your smiling faces make me feel better," I said, as I tousled his hair and kissed each of the boys on the cheek, instructing them to brush their teeth and get ready for bed.

Knowing that I still felt under the weather, James offered to put them to bed and read the bedtime story. While he finished tucking in the boys and praying with each of them, I offered up a quick prayer for boldness. "Honey," I began when he walked back into the kitchen, "I had an interesting dream a week ago, and I cannot get it out of my mind. Several things have happened this week that caused the dream to be even more difficult to forget."

9

"Well, what did you dream?" James queried, as we moved into the living room to snuggle on our faded blue sofa.

"I know this is going to sound really crazy, but I think God is trying to tell us something with this dream." I relayed every detail of the dream that I had tossed about in my mind all week and written about in my journal. I went on to tell him about the "coincidences" that had occurred, particularly and most significantly the phone call that evening that came during my time of prayer.

"Sweetheart, I don't think you're crazy," he said, tenderly stroking my arm. "And, I do believe that God sometimes speaks to His people in dreams; however, I believe that if God wants us to adopt a little girl, He will bring it about in His timing and in His way. He needs to lead us in this step-by-step, and we need to wait on Him."

Since I have always known my husband to have a spirit of discernment, I instantly knew that what he said was true for us. Couples unable to have children should certainly explore every option, including adoption. With three young children, even though I was unable to have any more, I knew James had responded correctly that we needed to wait on God. But I secretly believed he must have thought I was crazy. Knowing that God would bring a particular child into our lives would be the comfort and strength needed to help us through the challenges we would surely face. Nonetheless, I felt so ready, so expectant. I might as well have been pregnant because in my mind I knew God had given me this vision, had implanted it in my heart and would bring it to full term.

I felt so strongly about it that I wondered for a moment if my time of waiting to see God's fulfillment of this dream would occur like a pregnancy. "Mother's Day would be in nine months—that has to be it!" I thought. Something significant would happen on that day. I was so sure of it that my face surely exuded that pregnancy glow.

Our church's annual Mother-Daughter banquet approached, and I learned that neither my mother nor my mother-in-law would be able to attend. "No matter," I thought. The week before, I saw a doll wearing a dress that matched the one I wore, and James bought it for me. It had a watermelon-print dress with an adorable hat and became the second doll in my collection.

With doll in hand and a poem I had written for my future daughter, I attended the lovely banquet and shared with the ladies in our fellowship the dream I believed God had given me. Many ladies prayed for us that day, yet Mother's Day, my birthday and Christmas all passed without further direction from God and without a little girl. When each holiday came, my heart and mind imagined the various ways God might bring a daughter into our lives in time for that holiday. God's timing, God's way—I knew this truth, though it did not make it any easier to wait.

Not only did Christmas not bring a little girl into our family, it brought an unwelcome visitor, death. Christmas morning my husband's family came to celebrate Christmas for the first time in our home; previous years we had always observed Christmas Day in his parents' home. We all gathered in the living room near the twinkling tree, visiting, opening gifts, laughing and enjoying the morning. His family's tradition for opening gifts differed greatly from mine. My family had one person open a gift at a time, while everyone watched. This allowed everyone to join in the joy of the moment, and it made gift-giving and opening last a long time. This fit perfectly with my methodical personality. In James' family, everyone tore into their gifts at the same time. The boys, of course, favored this tradition. The race was on! Paper flew across the room while three boys, faces lit with excitement and joy, ripped into the gifts. Not wasting a moment of time, experienced toy handlers pulled gifts out of the packaging. Grandpa got down on the floor and tried out all the new toys right alongside them.

After the gifts had all been opened, the phone rang, bringing unsettling news. James' grandfather had been in the hospital with pneumonia; the call announced his passing. Smiles turned to solemn expressions as my husband, his parents, his sister and brother, and their spouses all left for the hospital. While James led his family in prayer and a reading from Psalms at the hospital, I began to pick up wrapping paper, bows and other remnants of an early-ended Christmas celebration. Our sons had never met their great-grandfather, who had only arrived in Texas a week earlier and went straight from the airport to the hospital. They did understand death, however, and asked "Mommy, is he in heaven?"

"Only God knows," I answered, silently praying for a way to redeem the joy of the morning. As if in answer to my prayer, an out-of-town relative showed up bringing squeals of delight from the boys. He showered them with gifts, Kolaches (a Czech pastry) and hours of rough-and-tumble on the floor.

Relieved that the boys' needs were being met, I prepared a cup of orange-spiced tea and sat down to ponder all that had just occurred. I foolishly wondered if God had forgotten the dream of little more than a year ago until I remembered His promise:

*"My child, I have not forgotten you. I will never
leave you or forsake you. You are written on the
palm of My hand."*

Parts of verses from Isaiah and Hebrews entered my
mind while God's Spirit spoke to my soul in response to
my thoughts. His Word always has a way of coming to my
mind just at the right time. The days following Christmas
left us contemplating our own short lives and awakened a
desire in us to live each day to its fullest.

On New Year's Eve, James reflected on the passing of
his grandfather, a rich man in terms of monetary wealth
but not rich in love, relationships or faith. We drove to our
little country church to attend the silent, candlelight New
Year's Eve midnight service. We took turns going inside to
pray while the other sat in the car with our three sleepy sons.
Instead of a usual service, people came into the candle-lit
sanctuary, picked up a prayer guide and sat quietly in the
presence of God. Worshipers could come and go at their
leisure between 11p.m. and 12:30 a.m., spending as much
time as they desired.

When we had both finished, James looked at me and
said, "Remember when we first met and looked into going
abroad, how we desired to do Christian humanitarian
development, following Jesus' example of serving others?
I think the time has come to pursue that again." Just after
midnight, with the boys asleep in the back seat, we drove
home quietly—each deep in thought.

New Year's Day dawned, bringing with it a renewed
desire in both my husband and me to make our lives count.
We knew God had bigger plans and a greater purpose for
our lives, but initially we had more questions than answers:
Where would we go and with what company? What would

we do? When would we leave? Would the boys go to school or would I home-school? In January 1998, even before all of those questions were answered, we knew the time had come to leave the comforts of America. We knew we would be overseas before the end of the year.

Throughout the year we made preparations for leaving: interviewing for a job, learning about the new country where we would be living, buying things we would need, making a will, getting vaccinations and selling our home and many of our belongings. To our amazement, our house out in the quiet countryside sold by owner within a few weeks of listing it.

Packing up was not a small task for us physically or emotionally. Having traveled all my life, since my father moved my three siblings and me from base to base in the Air Force, I had promised myself that whenever I got married I would stay in one place for the rest of my life! We had just bought this beautiful ranch-style home two years before. Yet it seemed right to go. God had been preparing all of us.

The week before we left the U.S., my friend Shelly had driven a couple of hours to come visit us where we were staying at my parents' home to say good-bye. Over the past five years, her three children and our three children had become best friends. Like stair steps, each of my sons had an age-mate in her son and daughters. Our children bundled up to fend off the frosty December air and headed for the outdoors. While we watched our children playing together in the tree house in my parents' backyard, I shared my burden with her that God had not yet answered my prayer regarding the dream He had given me.

Shelly took a sip of hot apple cider and set her mug on the end table beside the sofa. With all sincerity she said, "Perhaps God is not bringing a girl to you, but rather taking

14

you to your little girl." Tears welled up in my eyes at these words from my closest friend. This thought encouraged me greatly. Thankfully, God always sees a bigger picture, a tapestry that would hold many vibrant colors. Would one thread be that of a little girl?

TOO HARD

When waiting seems too hard to do,
When visions die,
When hopes fade,
You are there for me
And You care for me.
When waiting seems too hard to do,
When faith is weak,
When tears are strong,
You are here with me,
You stay near to me,
When waiting seems too hard!
--Delana1999

3. Heartbeat

Building my hope, on an unshakable Rock, I will not give up!

--Delana1999

My parents took us to the San Antonio International airport just a few days after Christmas 1998. We had packed about twelve bright red trunks and five carry-on bags, so it took a trailer to get us there. In those days (now that makes me sound old), guests could still accompany passengers to see them off at the gate. I still remember hugging my mom and seeing her smiling face (tears welling up in her eyes) when we passed through the gate to board the plane.

Before changing planes in Chicago, our carry-on bags passed through additional screening. We had filled one of the boys' bags completely with items to hold their attention on the long flight. Back then, airport security did not care about scissors, fingernail clippers or even pocket knives. Yet, the shape of one of those electronic fishing games caught the attention of the person viewing the screen, so someone had to open the bag to check the contents. We all stood around watching the security personnel unzip the bag revealing all kinds of toys for boys. With amused faces they sent us on our way to the gate for our international flight.

After two exhausting plane rides, we reached the island of Cyprus on December 29, 1998. Other Americans met us at the airport and drove us to a hotel. They had kindly purchased some American treats for us to snack on while we adjusted to the new time zone. Our sons especially enjoyed the Oreos, Pringles and Coca-cola.

We did not sleep well that first night; our body clocks were off, and the sound of honking filled our ears. In this country, people honked instead of using side and rearview mirrors. On the drive to our house, we noticed that all the buildings and houses were white, with flat rooftops where people placed plants, patio furniture and clothes-drying racks. Our first few months overseas came with many cultural adjustments to the Mediterranean lifestyle and local language, as well as difficulties in the lives of our family members back home: another grandparent died, a sibling went through a divorce and a parent struggled with cancer.

Throughout the year, James' IT job sent him on many trips to Central and South Asian countries to assist individuals and businesses with computer problems, as well as to teach hardware classes in schools started by Christian humanitarian companies. While traveling in Turkmenistan in the spring of 1999, he asked his translator about several similar buildings they passed on the road, buildings that resembled small schools. "Oh," Naya said several times, "that is another orphanage."

Struck by the number of orphanages in that city, James sent me the following e-mail: "Hi, Sweetheart! Before I forget I wanted to tell you that I think God may want us to come to this city to adopt a child. There are so many orphanages here. I'll tell you more when I get home. Love, James." Needless to say, he returned highly enthusiastic about adopting from this particular country. A friend from church introduced us to a lawyer who began to help us navigate local requirements for adopting. This included visits from the local equivalent of social services.

In November, James needed to make a return trip to Turkmenistan to teach a computer hardware course. This time he wanted me to go with him, so that we could visit orphanages and inquire about adoption. Thankfully, a good friend had agreed to take care of our boys so that I could accompany James on this journey.

Early during that visit, we contacted Naya to see if she could take us to orphanages and be our translator. We visited several locations and learned from one director that two young girls had been abandoned at a boys home. We tried to visit the boys home but the guard at the gate would not let us enter. Naya took us to the mayor who tried to discourage us from adopting in his country. He did, however, call the boys home and allow Naya to set up an appointment for us to visit the director. The director would only be available to meet with us towards the end of our ten day stay, two days prior to our departure. So, we traveled to a small town where James taught hardware classes, and I waited for time to pass.

Unfortunately, I had contracted food poisoning and Giardia, so I passed the time between the bed and the bathroom. When I was not sleeping or feeling miserable, I read my Bible study material on prayer and prayed. I had never felt so sick before, even with the morning sickness I experienced with all three of our sons. Thankfully, a Red Cross nurse in the town brought me some medication, and my condition began to improve. On my last two days in that town, I got to meet some of the students at the training center and slosh around the muddy bazaar in my galoshes.

We traveled by plane back to the capital city the day before our scheduled appointment with the orphanage director. That night, I prayed the following prayer, "Father God, if You would have us adopt one of these girls, then please let us know which one. If neither of these girls is part of Your plan for us, then close the door, before we even go out to the boys home."

The morning came and Naya arrived on time. "Would you please call the orphanage and make sure the guards at the gate are expecting us?" I asked. We knew that the boys home lay on a huge lot enclosed by a concrete wall with a guarded gate, and we wanted to be sure the guard knew to let us inside.

Naya's eyes grew dim and her face spoke volumes when she got off the phone with the receptionist at the boys home and said, "I am very, very sorry. They told me that the director just left the country and will not return for two weeks." We were scheduled to leave in two days.

I sunk to the floor, tears flooding my eyes. How could this be happening? I thought that surely this was the place and now was the time for God to answer our prayer regarding adoption. It had been three long years of waiting. How much longer could it take? The world was full of orphaned children in need of a loving family. "Why not ours? Why not now?" I thought. James put his arms around me, letting me release all of the many emotions that had been building inside my heart while we had waited the past week.

HOW

How can one unknown
Be loved so strong?
Will the hurts bring pain?
Will the nights bleed long?
Will my song forever be
A question floating on the sea
Of Tomorrow?
-- Delana©1999

As if Giardia and food poisoning were not enough, the initial feelings of discouragement and disappointment came over me like a wave of morning sickness. It seemed that our discouragement at this point had similarities to how people had described their feelings after a miscarriage.

Eventually, I remembered my prayer the night before. How could I not thank God for guarding our hearts? The pain and grief would have been much more severe if we had met these girls, then been denied the ability to adopt. God closed *this* door, but He had not said "no" to adoption. A mixture of gratefulness and sadness tugged at my heart. Suddenly, I missed our three sons greatly and longed to be reunited with them.

The first week back home, my prayer partner Teri and I met with one another. We had been going through a Bible study on prayer together. We studied the passage surrounding Matthew 7:7 which in the NASB reads: "Ask, and it will be given to you; seek, and you will find; knock, and it will be opened to you." We learned that the Greek form of those verbs more accurately translates: "Keep asking, and it will be given to you. Keep searching, and you will find. Keep knocking, and the door will be opened for you" (ISV). The study took us further in this line of thinking; we then read the parable Jesus told regarding prayer, persistence and not losing heart:

> *Luke 18:1-8 – ¹ Now He was telling them a parable to show that at all times they ought to pray and not to lose heart, ² saying, "In a certain city there was a judge who did not fear God and did not respect man. ³ There was a widow in that city, and she kept coming to him, saying, 'Give me legal protection from my opponent.' ⁴ For a while he was unwilling; but afterward he said to himself, 'Even*

though I do not fear God nor respect man, [5] yet because this widow bothers me, I will give her legal protection, otherwise by continually coming she will wear me out."' [6] And the Lord said, "Hear what the unrighteous judge said; [7] now, will not God bring about justice for His elect who cry to Him day and night, and will He delay long over them? [8] I tell you that He will bring about justice for them quickly. However, when the Son of Man comes, will He find faith on the earth?" (NASB)

Could I be persistent like this woman? Would the Son of Man find me faithful? Three years had passed since the dream. Doubts assailed me.

The following year, I struggled greatly with whether or not God had given me that dream and the strong desire I carried in my heart, but I decided to keep on keeping on. I would be the persistent widow. Or, rather, I would be the persistent *mother*!

One day, my friend Jill and I were out driving around. She was teaching me how to drive a stick-shift, something I had attempted to learn before, but at which I had never become proficient. Nor had I ever had such a thorough and patient instructor. Jill also had three children—two girls and a boy—just a little bit older than my children. That day, I shared with her the dream and the journey we had been traveling regarding adoption. After I finished, she smiled and replied, "Yeah, my husband and I have often thought it would be neat to adopt one day."

The way she spoke those words sounded like it would be great if it happened but fine, also, if it never came about—a passing thought for her. But, it was a deep, gut-wrenching passion for me—a God-given passion that would see me through this "pregnancy." At times, it had ceased to be waiting in anticipation, like a child waits for Christmas morning. It had become an ache, a groan, a raw emotion more similar to a starving person waiting for food.

Sometimes I found solace in talking with my husband, a close friend or a counselor. The best friends and counselors were not the ones who shared words of encouragement and verses of Scripture. The best friends and counselors knew that I knew those things; they just listened and cried with me.

Other times I cried out to God and looked for comfort in His Word, particularly in the Psalms. I found comfort in reading David's psalms, especially the ones where he expressed his anger and frustration. If he could do that and still receive God's love, then I could, too.

Once, God woke me up three times during the night with the reminder that He was the jealous lover of my soul. I weekly—sometimes daily—expressed my thoughts, prayers and poetry in my prayer journal.

WAITING

I will wait on You Lord.
I will wait to hear Your Word.
I want to know Your plan,
To wait for Your command.
I will be still and wait.
Your truth I seek to know,
Before I act, before I go.
I will listen,
I will follow,
I will wait.
I will wait expectantly.
In Your Word I will believe.
I will run the race.
I will seek Your face.
I will be still and wait.
I will hope in Your name,
Giving thanks, all the same.
I will listen,
I will follow,
I will wait.
--Delana2000

4. False Contractions

"For My thoughts are not your thoughts, Nor are your ways My ways," declares the LORD (Isaiah 55:8 NASB).

After spending nearly two years in Cyprus, we decided to work for a Christian humanitarian organization in Azerbaijan, a country similar to and just across the Caspian Sea from Turkmenistan, the country we had just visited. Once again we packed up all our belongings, said good-bye to dear friends and took our three boys—aged six, eight and ten—to a new country. We arrived in September 2000, in time for the boys to start school and for another Christmas to pass.

Though unsure about another move, the boys seemed excited about this new adventure. The adventure over the next four years included watching fire-jumpers, eating mountain oysters, climbing cliffs while precariously hanging over rushing water, swimming in hot and cold springs, splashing under waterfalls, learning a new language, experiencing an earthquake and much more; however, that could fill another book. I will let my sons tell that story.

During the busyness of our first year there, heightened by language learning and a medical trip out of the country to have my gall-bladder removed, time passed without too much longing for God to answer my prayer. Not having much down time kept my mind from being consumed with thoughts and emotions regarding adoption. However, anytime I saw a little girl I caught myself day-dreaming of what it would be like to have a daughter. Well-meaning friends would tell me: "You have three sons; one day you will have three daughters when they get married." Maybe so, but that did not come close to easing the ache my heart held for a little girl.

Others would say: "You will be blessed with granddaughters!" Did they have the ability to foretell my future? How would they know? What if I only had grandsons or no grandchildren at all? Still others tried to comfort me by telling me about all of the "spiritual" daughters I had. None of these thoughts made the burden for a daughter any lighter.

In the spring of 2001, I attended a conference in Istanbul, Turkey, for Christian expatriate women. While there, I ran in to some old friends who were excited to tell me something: "Delana, we have some great news to tell you about Jill. She just adopted a little baby boy!" I should have been excited when I discovered that an abandoned baby now had a wonderful and loving family. However, my heart first turned to anger. Thankfully, God can handle our anger as evidenced by David's Psalms:

Psalm 13:2--How long must I wrestle with my thoughts and every day have sorrow in my heart? How long will my enemy triumph over me? (NIV)

Psalm 42:9--I will say to God my rock, "Why have You forgotten me? Why do I go mourning because of the oppression of the enemy? (NASB)

Psalm 31:10--My life is consumed by anguish and my years by groaning; my strength fails because of my affliction, and my bones grow weak. (NIV)

"Oh God, why? Why? Jill had a passing thought about adoption, and You practically placed this baby in her lap. I have been passionately praying and longing and seeking You for a daughter to adopt, and I am greeted by closed doors. Why?"

I wanted to be happy for Jill, but my heart ached. I wondered if this bore any similarity to what a woman longing to give birth to a child felt every time another friend became pregnant. Or, what a woman who desires to be married feels every time one of her friends gets married. She wants to be genuinely happy for her friend or relative, and yet a gnawing, raw ache in the pit of her stomach makes her wonder why it cannot be her. My friends rebuked me for my inability to rejoice for Jill. They were right; it was wrong for me to be angry at her blessing. Yet I praised God that He loved me even through my pain and sorrow, even through my frustration and fear.

Five months later an unforgettable event occurred that changed the world. Sitting in a local friend's living room in a downtown bustling city of millions, I sat laughing, talking and celebrating the upcoming wedding of a very dear friend. She was having her henna party. Women of all ages packed out the small room to decorate the bride-to-be and themselves with the reddish-brown dye. Dancing, eating, laughing and rejoicing filled the evening. Suddenly, my friend's brother arrived home with a grim expression and turned on the television. After I saw the surreal images of the planes crashing into the twin towers and received hugs from all attending the bridal shower, my husband called and said that I should return to our apartment. I left immediately.

My husband and three sons sat watching the news in our living room. We seemed so far away. We were. Our neighbors—compassionate and caring Muslim women and men—came over and asked about our family back in the U.S. They also called us for days, "Is your family okay? Was anyone there? Did you have friends there? Are you sure everyone is okay? We are sorry for what these evil men have done." Our friends and neighbors had experienced wars, the deaths of loved ones and suffering. They cared about us and our family and were ready to empathize with us during the tragedy of 9/11.

Our family then began to call: "Have you seen the news? Are you safe?" Yes. We were safe. They were safe. But many Americans were not. Many were directly touched by loss, by pain; they came together and held each other up through the pain.

I realized more and more that my focus had gotten off track. I focused on a dream, instead of on the Giver of Dreams. I had started reading the book *The Journey of Desire* by John Eldredge. This book blessed me, encouraged me and helped me understand God and myself in new ways. In this book, Eldredge compares burying our desires to the servant who buried the talent in the ground instead of investing it. He equated an inability to trust God with a desire to a lack of faith. And, at the same time, I learned of needing to place a higher importance on my communion with God. Throughout my reading and prayer time, I had begun to wonder if I might need to lay down my desire for a daughter and trust God to replace that desire with Himself.

Living in a developing nation exhausted me. I shopped daily for food, walking one mile round trip, stopping in several tiny shops to find the things we needed. Some days it took stopping at several shops to find a single roll of toilet paper. Many locals at that time prefered to use water from a watering can or sprayer instead of using toilet paper, so it was not high on their list of things to keep stocked.

People crowded the sidewalks and honking cars crowded the roads. Buying produce required the tiring act of negotiating, something I never developed a knack or appreciation for, even though my husband loved it! We lived in an old concrete block apartment, badly in need of a new coat of paint. The boys and I carried groceries up three flights of stairs, often holding our noses in order not to gag on the strong urine smell that frequently permeated the stairwell in our building. Since the boys stayed upstairs with their language tutor while I shopped, it usually worked this way: I pulled my little red cart around to all the shops within a mile from home. Then, approaching the bottom of our stairwell, I used a walkie-talkie to let my sons know I had returned and needed their help.

I learned to prepare all kinds of foods from scratch, since biscuit, pancake and cake mixes did not exist there; ready-made goods such as tortillas, bagels and English Muffins were also unavailable. We poured water into a bucket filtering system several times a day for drinkable water, and we hung laundry out from our third-floor apartment window.

One day while I attended a funeral service in the home of my downstairs neighbor, I saw a ghostly apparition—my bed linens—flying by the window and down to the muddy ground below. I promptly excused myself to rescue my belongings from the alleyway behind our building. We purchased a small clothes dryer after that, which left the neighbors quite curious. One neighbor asked me if she could buy some sheets for us. When I asked her why, she responded, "I don't see your linens hanging from your window anymore and thought that perhaps you needed new ones." With so many other responsibilities—raising children, learning language, teaching English to adults—I soon learned that I needed help.

A friend introduced me to a learning-challenged lady in her 30s who needed a part-time job doing housework. Merry began coming to our home for a few hours once a week to help me out. After a few weeks, I learned why she lost the job she had at an orphanage: she worked very slowly. She did a good job, though, and willingly worked for pay by the job rather than by the hour. At some point during our second year, Merry invited me to visit her former place of employment—one of the city orphanages.

"Sure," I said, "I'd love to." What was I thinking? Trusting God with my desires and laying them at his feet was one thing, but putting myself into a home full of children who needed a mommy was something else altogether! I would want to take home every little girl that I saw!

The words had come out of my mouth, though, so I had to follow through and go to the orphanage with Merry. First, we walked through a playroom where boys and girls aged three to five lined the walls. Some played with worn-out toys, some sat staring blankly out into the room, some drooled, some cried, and some smelled awful. One little energetic four-year-old girl came up to me smiling and shook my hand. Then, she started jumping around and teasing playfully with me. Before I left the room, however, she came up to me angrily and blurted out in her own language, "I'm going to set you on fire!" Now *that* scared me. [A year later, an American family adopted this little girl.]

Merry and I moved on to the baby room. Cribs lined the room and filled the middle, end to end. A worker came into the room on schedule to prop up bottles in the mouths of all the babies and to change diapers (whether needed or not, but most often they were long overdue). No one really held the babies. Many of the babies had given up on crying because they learned that crying did not achieve the desired result of getting food, getting changed or being held. I walked down the rows of cribs looking in at each child. One baby girl cooed and smiled when I looked into her crib. Once I passed out of view, she began to cry. I backed up and looked in her crib, once again evoking the same reaction from her—a smile and coo. Later, I wondered why I did not pick her up. Maybe I feared attaching my heart to a child who could not be mine. I left the orphanage with a mix of emotions: fear, anger, love, desire, sorrow, longing.

A couple of months before our second Christmas in Azerbaijan, James and I had the opportunity to attend an incredible marriage conference. Two couples came from the U.S. to work with small groups of English-speaking expatriates. On the last night of the conference, a friend we had met approached us and said, "I heard that you might want to adopt. Is that true?"

We had not shared that information with more than a couple of people; we were trying to step back and let God lead. Was this from God? Not sure how to answer the woman, I said, "Uh…why do you ask?"

"Three American couples, including my husband and me, started the adoption process here. We have a friend from the U.S. who will come next month to do our home-studies at no charge, but we have agreed to pay her travel expenses. We want to know if you want to be a part of this?" she asked as James and I gave each other puzzling looks.

Knowing that we had already purchased tickets for a three-month trip to the U.S. for two weeks after the social worker's planned visit, we said, "Let us pray about it and call you in a couple of days." We knew that home studies were only good for one year, and we had not yet started the process with any agency or orphanage or government worker. We had no particular child in mind and no direction from God.

"This opportunity found us!" I told my husband. "Do you think it is a God-thing?" I wondered if this could be the signs of a child on the way.

"It does sound pretty incredible," James replied, "but let's give it some time and really pray about it." The woman did not need an answer until two to three days later.

We strongly desired to hear from God. We did not want to make a costly investment of time and money if we were not going to be able to complete the process of adoption prior to the expiration of a home study. Was this an open door from God? We prayed that God would close the door if it was not from Him.

Once again I turned to writing and poured my emotions out on paper. On December 14, 2001, I recorded the following thoughts in my prayer journal:

> *Father God, I am too emotionally weak to make wise decisions. You know that they want us to help pay for the airfare of the woman doing the home study. You must direct our steps. How could I so easily fall back into this? Is it what You desire—or am I sinning against You by resurrecting my desire? Please open or close doors as You feel is best.*
>
> *I know You love me and that Your plan for our lives is best. My heart is a tumult of emotions. My heart has been freshly laid open. It is bleeding. I do not know what to do but I will trust You and follow You. You are my healer. "Even when I am afraid, I keep on trusting You. You have kept record*

of my days of wandering. You have stored my tears
in your bottle and counted each of them" (Psalm
56:3, 8 CEV).

The next day our new friend called us to say, "The social worker has had to make a scheudle change. She will still be coming, but she will come a month later than her originally planned visit. Are you still interested?"

SLAM! Another door closed. We had already purchased tickets for our upcoming flight to America. We would no longer be in the country when the social worker was scheduled to arrive. We thought that we had entered the final trimester and labor was approaching. Unfortunately, these were only false contractions.

Turning to my Heavenly Father and Comforter, I sought refuge in the Psalms and in the words of a poem I had previously written.

REVISION
A dream lost is to die a little
a little more, a little less
a brittle, bitter ending
descending upon my heart,
tearing at my soul,
wearing at my ability
to go on.
Until a song
rises forth singing of
newer visions, undenied hope
not erasing or replacing
the aching of my deepest part
but causing my own soul to carry on.
--Delana2001

Delana H. Stewart

God had honored our prayer, guarded our hearts and finances, and He let us know that this was not the right time. I began to wonder, however, if "not now" really meant "not ever." Six years had now passed since the conception of the dream. It seemed so unfair that thousands of children needing parents could lie poorly cared for in orphan homes, while we so desired to open our hearts and home to a child. "Why, God? Why? I don't understand!"

> _December 19, 2001—Lord God, I thank You for clearly showing us that we are not to be a part of this home study. "When I said, 'My foot is slipping,' your love, O Lord, supported me. When anxiety was great within me, Your consolation brought joy to my soul" (Psalm 94:18, 19 NIV). I need you, Lord. Continue to hold me, comfort me and bring my peace. Guard my heart. Wipe my tears. Thank you for the tenderness of my husband and for children who love me dearly._

> _December 27, 2001—Father, I am your daughter. You know my heart. I do want Your way. Your way is always better than my own. In guiding me down Your path, help my heart not hurt so much and not long for that which cannot be mine. You know of my longings for a daughter. Heal my broken heart. Help me onward._

34

5. Bed Rest

"For the vision is yet for the appointed time; It hastens toward the goal and it will not fail. Though it tarries, wait for it; For it will certainly come, it will not delay" (Habakkuk 2:3 NASB).

Time spent with family and friends in the U.S. renewed us physically and emotionally. We returned to Central Asia mid-2002 ready for another two years with people we had grown to love and considered our second family. We returned to the third floor of the tenement-style apartment block in a city of millions. James continued to teach computer and business courses while I taught English part-time and tutored co-workers' children.

Deep inside, I still greatly struggled with unanswered prayer. Even though it was Hannah's barrenness in the Old Testament book of 1 Samuel that caused her to grieve, I could resonate with her emotions and spirit while she poured her heart out to God—waiting year after year for His favorable reply. At one point, Eli, the priest, thought Hannah was drunk. *"Not so, my lord," Hannah replied, "I am a woman who is deeply troubled. I have not been drinking wine or beer; I was pouring out my soul to the LORD"* (I Sam 1:15 NIV).

Like Hannah, I had my own song I poured out to the Lord . . .

RESTING

I will rest in the Hand that never fails me.
I cry because my hopes are crushed,
yet I will trust Thee.
Though my heart's prayer remains unanswered,
I will not doubt.
Your love may deny me the thing
for which I cry out.
I will believe in the Hand that saves,
Though troubles break like storm-tossed waves,
And disappointment stings like an angry bee,
Yet, in You, I will believe.
My tears fall like rain upon a weary land.
My soul is buffeted by the wind, and
I still find rest in the Hand that never fails me.
Though my longing cries out
from deep within my soul,
I will not doubt, because I know
The Hand that made the wave calmed the sea.
--Delana2001

At some point, after returning from Texas, I continued reading Eldredge's book *The Journey of Desire*. After putting the boys to bed, I would retreat to our tiny bedroom. The room barely contained our dresser and queen-sized bed. With my side of the bed crammed up against the wall, there was just enough room to close the door. Many evenings, I lay on the bed reading Eldredge's book until I could no longer keep my eyes open. Through that book and my prayer time, I felt both affirmed in the desire to adopt a daughter and yet troubled that the desire was becoming an idol. I wrestled with God over this matter for weeks.

Would God give me a vision, a dream, a desire and then ask me to give it up? Put it to death? "Well," I supposed, "God did give Abraham a vision, a promise of a son, and then the actual son, but He still asked Abraham to lay that son on the altar." Did Abraham trust God? Did Abraham love God more? Did I love the dream, the desire—dare I say—*the promise* of a daughter more than I loved God? Was the desire for God to answer my prayer taking God's place in my heart? I placed my well-worn journal between the mattress and the concrete wall and went to sleep.

Days, weeks and months passed. I gave the desire back to God. I lay it down. Put it to death. Or, so I thought. Many times during those two years I found myself picking it back up, struggling with finding peace in giving up the desire. But I loved God more. So, I filled pages of my journal with these thoughts revealing the battle that waged within my heart:

Why did I pray for a miracle? Why did I fast?
Why did I hold fast, hang on, keep hoping?
Why did I pray believing and believe that You had answered?
Why does my heart hurt so badly?
Why must we pray and pray and pray believing and hoping that all things are possible?
Why can't I give up?

Then at other times, I began to grasp the truth that God knows the pain of letting go. He understands the tug-of-war. Doesn't He?

But You understand. Don't you?
Did You die a thousand deaths,
when they hung you on the tree?
When the blood flowed from your side,
And you cried,

"My God, my God, why have you forsaken me?"
Did You feel abandoned by the One who gave you life,
By the One who taught you how to dream,
the One who gave You hope?
Did You feel He could not hear You, was not near You?
Did You fear for just a moment
that He may never look upon you again?
And, that He would never say, "This is my Son, whom I love
And with whom I am pleased?"
Did You think the pain would never end?
Did You lose hope?
Did You think the enemy had won?
(Even though You knew he wouldn't win in the end.)
Did You feel defeated?
Did Your dream die? Did You cry? Did You feel my tears . . .
From well before my years began to be?

I knew that this unfulfilled desire did not begin to compare with the pain of a miscarriage or stillbirth, but six to seven years of "pregnancy" now lay on the altar to be sacrificed. My heart was raw. Yet, I desired to love God more.

Can I have a different dream?
Can I have a new prayer to pray for and believe in?
Is there one that You will answer?
Can you show me Your desire? Can you make it mine?
Does it have to take too long?
Do I have to love too much?
Can it be fulfilled?
Tomorrow?
And You said, "Come to me, all you who are weary and burdened, and I will give you rest" (Matthew 11:28 NIV).
Here I am. I have come.

I am weary and heavy laden.
Do You have rest for my soul, today? Tomorrow?
Until You return?
Do You see me now, even now, as I pour out my soul to
You?
Do You hear me now, even now, as my heart groans?
Will You touch me, touch my spirit, in a way only You can?
You are the Source and beginning of my life!
Lord God, You are Holy!
Life is not about me.
Life is about living for You.
When I get caught up with
my needs, my hopes, my dreams, my problems,
help me to remember that life is about You!
Show me the things You most desire from me.
 --HeartSongs, Delana2002-2004

Many things filled those two years—good things. The English and Computer training center blossomed into over 200 students per semester. By fall of 2003, James and one of his students took his computer training program out into villages and refugee areas to help those who could not afford to come into the city. Our sons grew and matured, developed many friendships, spoke like the locals and enthusiastically embraced life. I enjoyed teaching my English students, visiting and praying with neighbors and learning to cook local dishes. My walk with the Lord grew, and my heart began to find rest.

Late in 2003 James and I explored the possibility of moving to and working in another country. We were unsure where we would go or what we would do, but we felt it might be time to do something different since the boys were getting older. One of the possible job locations included a country in the Middle East that we had barely heard about—the United Arab Emirates (U.A.E.).

In the spring of 2004 I became quite ill, and the doctors could only narrow down the possibilities but not fully diagnose or treat me where we lived. Only one country relatively near us—the U.A.E.—had the capability to determine for sure what I had. Was it a coincidence? We did not think so, and we praised God that this illness gave us the nudge we needed to explore an opportunity outside of our comfort zones.

In March, James and I traveled to the U.A.E. so that the doctors could examine me and find out what caused the symptoms, while each of our boys stayed with a different friend. We visited various hospitals before I received the diagnosis of sub-acute thyroiditis. In other words, my thyroid had an infection. Since it was not Grave's disease or some other thyroid issue requiring surgery, my thyroid would heal on its own over the course of a year.

During the rest of our time in the Middle East, James interviewed for a job, and we learned about the schools, shopping, people and culture. The U.A.E. was not a melting pot of people, but it was a tossed salad. Everywhere we went we saw people from countries all over the world including the Philippines, Jordan, Egypt, Pakistan, India, U.K, France, U.S., Korea and gulf Arab countries. The grocery markets, clothing stores and restaurants reflected the diversity seen on the streets.

After returning to Central Asia, we talked with our sons about their thoughts regarding another move. Though they had grown quite attached to the people of Azerbaijan—and to expatriate friends—their sense of adventure urged them onward; the Spirit's hand upon them gave them peace. Many people there had become like parents and grandparents and siblings to all of us. Packing up and preparing to leave included many good-bye dinners as well as excursions to favorite places.

For me, it also meant death of a vision—laying down my dream and desiring God more. I could survive without knowing why the doors to my dream always closed; I could not survive without the love, grace, and nearness of my Lord.

Years of persevering in prayer, waiting for God to answer, waiting for Him to fulfill a dream, I reached a point where the dream had to die. At that time, I sincerely thought that the dream died, the door closed forever, never to be opened again. But, the story did not end there; like a seed it fell into the ground dead, in order to spring forth and bloom. The dead of winter had come before the new life of spring.

God had shown me that I needed to choose. Continuing to serve my desire and allowing it to consume me hindered my prayer life. The sin of idolizing my dream kept His presence and His power from being what He wanted it to be in my life. I could not go on without a fervent, powerful, unhindered prayer life with my Lord. I did not need a daughter, but I would suffer greatly if my prayer life remained hindered.

I decided right then to pack up all the "treasures" that I had set aside for a daughter, all the reminders of my desire. I had been keeping an adoption story diary in which I had written thoughts during the journey, a diary that I had one day intended on giving to my daughter. I wrote one final entry in that book to be packed with those other items. This is what I had written–

> *Today, I surrender my desire for a daughter to God.*
> *I need God, my Father. I need His warm embrace.*

I need to know He is near. I need to know that He hears me. I trust He knows what is best for me. I will no longer seek adoption. My desire for a daughter became so great that it became for me an idol. I only serve the Mighty God. His love for me is great! I cannot bear His discipline. I need Him to hear me. I pray that as He has asked me to lay down my desire for a daughter, that He will remove all longings for a daughter from my heart and fill up the void space with His love. It is hard to let this go, as it has been a prayer journey and a part of my life for many years. Today, this part of me is being removed, cut off, pruned by the Master Gardener to make room for more of God, more of His power, more of His love and Presence in my life.

That was the darkness before the dawn.

In August of 2004, we took up residence in the U.A.E. Not only was a new day dawning, but we had the opportunity to experience a new country, new people, new foods, new sights, sounds and smells. We saw God's hand at work in our lives and found rest in knowing that His plans are good. I no longer cried out to God for a daughter. I no longer ached every time I saw a little girl. I truly rested in my Father's hands. A new peace that truly passed all understanding floated down from heaven and landed on me.

These thoughts that I had previously written in my prayer journal encouraged me, lifted me up . . .

SUSPENDED

Going beyond an answer
Knowing You
When fears fly high
When eyes don't dry
And I no longer can
You stand.
And I too weak to grasp
Your hand
Allow Your breath to suspend my soul.
--Delana2000

6. Contractions

*"For I know the plans I have for you," declares the LORD, "plans to prosper you and not to harm you, plans to give you hope and a future"
(Jeremiah 29:11 NIV).*

Texas summers had clearly not prepared us for the extremely hot temperatures we faced that first month in the Middle East. Or perhaps having lived in a colder climate the past four years in Central Asia desensitized us to hot, balmy weather. Thankfully, our house had ceramic tile floors, concrete walls and air conditioning. The large trees in the backyard also provided some shade to our kitchen and dining area during the heat of the day.

Living only a few minutes' walk from the beach, the boys—now 10, 12, and 14—enjoyed building sand castles while James and I took moonlit strolls along the shore in the warm salty water. Our sons continued to amaze me in their ability to travel to new places; with joy and enthusiasm they learned to appreciate new people, new languages and new cultures. Thoughts of adopting a daughter were laid to rest; I poured myself into studying language, learning my way around and developing relationships with neighbors. I deeply desired to be the hands and feet of Jesus to those around me. During this time I wrote verses to a song for which I had written the following chorus a few years earlier.

*Let your love, wash over me
Let your Spirit descend
Fill me up, and lead me on*

Let your love, flow through me.
--Delana2001

In December, a heart-wrenching event occurred that shook the world—the 2004 Indian Ocean earthquake and tsunami. Mighty waves (nearly 100 feet high) crashed the shores of Thailand, Indonesia, India and Sri Lanka demolishing thousands of homes and killing more than 230,000 people. The original 9-9.3 magnitude earthquake caused a domino effect of earthquakes nearly halfway around the world. This devastation affected families in at least 14 countries. My heart went out to all the people who suffered loss, particularly the children who lost mothers, fathers, sisters, brothers, neighbors and friends. While this event triggered an emotional response around the world, prompting donations exceeding $14 billion, it did not rekindle in me the desire to adopt a child. Our children had grown, and God had healed my heart.

In January 2005 our family traveled to Thailand for an education conference and much needed vacation. Teri, my prayer partner from 1999, had moved to Thailand with her family and asked us to come over for dinner. Three days before heading home, we ate dinner with Teri's family and celebrated our youngest son's eleventh birthday. After finishing dinner, we moved to the living room to enjoy chocolate cake and hot tea and try to catch up on four years of each other's lives. At one point in the conversation, Teri asked, "Are you guys still thinking about adopting?"

My heart skipped a beat, but my mind and mouth quickly replied, "Well, a lot has happened; much time has passed. Our boys are older now, and we feel like the time has come to let that dream go and move on." James put his arm around me. He knew that it had been a long, hard journey, and I would need his strength just to talk about it.

Teri paused a bit and took a sip of her tea, then said, "Well, I really feel burdened to at least tell you why I asked. You see, a friend of mine here has a foster home for babies and young children. One little girl has been in her foster home for many years and will turn five years old soon. They thought a family in Australia would adopt her, but it looks like the adoption may fall through. If no one adopts her, then she will have to go into the government home and girls' school. While we prayed about her situation just the other day, you came to my mind."

Teri asked me to come up stairs with her for a few minutes. When we got up there, I confessed, "Teri, I'm afraid. This feels kind of like Pandora's Box. I think that if I open up to this possibility it will only rekindle desire I have laid to rest. And, if I open up to the desire only to have another door close, I'm not sure I can be strong enough to handle it. Yet, at the same time I am afraid that if I don't pursue this, then I may always wonder if this was the moment I was supposed to have faith and didn't."

"Delana," she said, "remember in the past when you prayed that God would close the door and guard your heart if it was not from Him? God is a God of faith, not fear. At least give Him the same opportunity to show you if this is from Him."

Knowing that Teri's friend had 9-10 foster children and several biological children, and knowing that we were leaving in two days, I agreed to give God a chance to open or close this door. I also knew that James would support me in this. We sat on the edge of a bed and closed our eyes. Even though my heart ached at the thought of possible disappointment ahead, I prayed: "Dear God, if this is an open door from You and will lead to a daughter being brought into our family, please let this lady have time tomorrow morning to meet with me. If this would only lead to false hope, please close this door right now and let tomorrow not be a good day for her to have me come over."

After saying "Amen," Teri picked up the phone and called her friend, who invited me to come over around ten in the morning. A little while later, our family left Teri's home with mixed emotions: excited, expectant, nervous and unsure what to expect.

The next morning James hung out with the boys at the hotel pool while Teri took me to her friend's house. I walked into the playroom and sat down on the floor with several children aged two to four. Helpers came in and out of the room. They played with the children, sang songs, laughed and saw to their needs—and to the needs of the babies in the other room. Joy filled the room, and I knew that this family and their helpers loved and cared for these children and babies.

Upon meeting the particular four-year-old girl that Teri had been praying about, two things instantly came to mind: (1) I could so easily fall in love with this child and make her my daughter and (2) this child was not to be mine. I do not know how I knew that, but I had a joy and a peace all at once. I am so thankful God revealed that to me because six months later her adoption to Australia came through after all. During the visit, I learned that at that time Americans could adopt directly through Thai Social Services without hiring an agency. I left that morning with hope and with information that could help us get started if we decided to do so.

That night James and I researched more about the adoption process in Thailand using several websites I

48

had jotted down in the morning. One thing troubled us: many of the sites said that it could take one to two years to complete the process. We had already waited so long. We really did not want to wait two more years! The fact that many countries open and close to foreign adoptions and frequently change the rules also concerned us. (A year or two later adoptions from Thailand would fall under the Hague Convention, which has made the process even more difficult.) After researching and praying, we agreed to at least visit with the Thai Consul when we returned to the Middle East.

On the plane ride home a name came to my mind— Jade. This precious green stone was popular in Thailand and used for many things. In the night market, vendors sold bracelets, earrings, little elephants and many other items made from jade. It also struck me that JA came from the first two letters in James' name and DE came from the first two letters in my name. I shared this with James, and he liked it (another miracle . . . that we would agree on a name). If the past eight years were something like eight months of pregnancy, then this was the first real contraction.

More contractions followed upon our return home. Before the month of February finished, we had visited the Thai Embassy to discuss what it would take for us to adopt from Thailand. We also discussed the timetable since the one to two years listed on the Internet concerned us. To this the Thai Consul replied, "Oh, no, it will not take so long. Right now the welfare department processes adoptions within six months of receiving the application." This gave us the courage to go ahead and start the process with Thailand. What we did not know (and he did not know) was that the shortened six-month process was only for Thai citizens wanting to adopt children left orphaned by the Tsunami.

The Thai Consul, a young, soft-spoken, kind-hearted man came to our home to complete the Thai home study as part of the process. "Why do you want to adopt when you already have three children?" he asked. (He was not the first and certainly not the last person to ask us this.)

How do we answer this question? Would he believe God gave me a dream eight years ago? Would it even matter to him? My mouth felt full of cotton and my hand, tucked inside of James', must have felt clammy at this point. While my mind raced through all the possible ways to reply, James squeezed my hand and said, "My wife cannot have any more children, and we have always wanted a daughter. A daughter will make our family complete."

The Thai Consul smiled and continued making notes about our family and home, where we had lived, what our childhoods were like, how we met, what kind of education we had, and what our financial situation was. He talked with each of our sons, and then we gave him a tour of our home, discussing our plans for where our daughter would sleep. Leaving our home, he seemed content that we could provide a good home for a little girl.

By April, we had submitted our application, financial statements and home study. By August, the receipt of our FBI fingerprints completed the application process. Now our application would join the stack of others waiting to be processed.

The temperatures showed no sign of relief and perhaps even continued to climb as did the heavy humidity. Once a week, my new prayer partner and I would either walk on the beach or meet in a coffee shop to share our concerns and lift each other up. It was definitely an indoor kind of a day. We ordered our coffee and claimed some overstuffed, comfortable chairs by the window, where we could look out and watch the waves wash up on the shore.

"How is the adoption process coming along?" Rachel asked.

"Well, I think we have done everything we can do at this point," I replied.

Nearly as desperate for information about the process as I, Rachel asked, "What happens next?"

The social worker in Thailand had explained it to the Thai Consul who explained it to us. Now I shared that same information with Rachel, "First, our social worker Ana must present our application to the adoption review board for them to approve us to adopt. Then, once approved, she will locate a child who matches our request (a girl aged four to six) and ask the review board if they approve the referral. Once she has located a child to recommend, she will send us some brief information about that child. If we want more information, she will send us more. Each time we say 'yes,' she will send us more details and then a picture. If at any time we say 'no,' she will go back to the review board for a new referral. If after receiving all the information about a child we say 'yes,' then Ana will present our file and the child's file at a meeting of the adoption review board for them to approve the match and issue us an invitation to come to Thailand. At that time, we will spend time with the child and meet with the review board one final time."

"Wow! Sounds extensive," Rachel exclaimed. "If the first child is not the right child for your family, it sounds like the process could take a really long time."

"Yes, and that concerns me." I said.

"Well, let's begin praying right now that the very first referral will be God's choice for you," she said. We took time right there in the coffee shop to commit the whole situation to God, trusting Him to guide the whole process.

September, October and November of 2005 passed, and each time I called Ana I got the same response, "Your case has not yet been presented for approval. The Adoption review board only meets twice a month, and the first priority goes to families who have come to pick up their children. When time allows, social workers can then present matches for approval. Finally, we can present new applications. Sorry I do not have more news for you yet."

Another December came, and we decorated our home to prepare for Christmas. Our traveling 2½ foot tall Christmas tree sat on a table in one corner of the room with nativity figurines displayed in front of the tree. Garland and lights hung in the windows and doorways. We even hung an extra stocking in honor of the little girl who would one day celebrate Christmas with us. One week before Christmas we received some exciting news, and on December 31, 2005, I sent the following e-mail to my friend Teri:

> *"About a week before Christmas we got news from Ana that we have finally been approved by the Adoption Review Board. She says that they placed us on the waiting list (which means the waiting list committee has our application in a stack of I don't know how many others). She said that she may not have any new information before March, but that I could check on the status in February. I'll be checking in February.*
>
> *Wish it wasn't more waiting . . . but I'm sure she will be worth the wait. This committee that has our application now is the one that is supposed to be matching families to waiting children."*

At the moment we received the news, my water broke. Nine years of pregnancy had passed and now labor and delivery could begin. I sat down on our balcony soaking in the view of the neighbors' flowers. Journal and pen in hand, I expressed my praise to the One who had brought us this far and would bring it about in His timing.

THE PALM

From my bedroom window
Between two, white plastered houses,
Stands the stately date palm
High above it all—
And down the wall,
Cascading fuchsia
Bougainvillea
Like a waterfall.
Weathering
Summer heat,
Winter winds,
The stately palm
Waves its limbs
Shouting
Hallelujahs
To its Maker
The King.
--Delana2005

7. Labor

*"A woman giving birth to a child has pain because
her time has come; but when her baby is born she
forgets the anguish because of her joy that a child is
born into the world"(John 16:21 NIV).*

I spent more than twelve hours in labor with my firstborn
son, Josh—the entire day of my husband's birthday. "Happy
Birthday, Dear!" Our son, exerting his wishes to have
his own special day, finally came into the world the next
morning at 1 a.m. However, with a nine *year* pregnancy,
would this labor process be long or short? Twelve weeks?
Twelve months? How long until our little girl would be in
our arms?

We rang in 2006 with friends and stayed busy with
our jobs. In addition to homeschooling our three sons, I
supported many families that were homeschooling abroad
by answering their questions via e-mail, sending monthly
newsletters and praying for them. Still, January could not
pass quickly enough. I did not want to rush Ana by calling
February 1st, so I gave her a week before finally calling her
on February 8th.

"Hi, Ana, this is Delana. You suggested I call in February
to see if you had any news for us regarding a referral."

"I am sorry. We have plenty of healthy boys in the four-
to six-year-age range, but the only healthy girl in that range
has been matched to the family ahead of you. You have three
children so we cannot give you first priority. You can check
back in two months if you like," she added.

I really do not remember how I replied, but I am sure it included a deep sigh and heaviness of heart. Ana then said, "Are you willing to consider girls with special needs? If you are, that could improve the priority of your being matched."

She gave us more details, which I included in an e-mail I sent to many friends that very day:

> *"They have a seven-year-old girl with an IQ of 80, and they also have several three- to five-year-old girls who had the cleft lip operation. It is a lot to think and pray about.*
>
> *For instance, we are praying about being open to the following: a child who has a complex medical history, but no currently known medical concerns; a child who is not meeting her developmental milestones on target; a child born prematurely or who had moderately low birth weight; a child with a cleft lip that has been operated on before the child turned 5 years old; and a child with vision impairment in one eye (or mild vision problems in both eyes)."*

After praying and talking with our sons, researching various needs, talking with friends who are doctors, counselors and foster parents, we decided to contact Ana before February ended to let her know that we would adopt a girl with mild special needs. We also extended the age range from 4-6 to 3-7. During that phone call, Ana replied, "Your first adoption profile should arrive in less than two months."

When my mother's birthday rolled around on April 19, 2006, two months had passed since I had last spoken with

Ana. After another very disappointing phone call, I once again e-mailed my friends and family:

> *"Okay . . . I'm very discouraged now! In February, when Ana said 'less than two months,' she should have said 'Inshallah' (If God wills).*
>
> *I talked with her today and was told to check back May 17th (after the next time the matching committee meets). I'm disappointed . . . to say the least. I wish I would stop being as naive as to believe that I can take people for their word.*
>
> *And for some reason God thinks that He hasn't given us more than we can bear . . . but today I have to wonder about that. Please pray for us."*

Unfortunately, James had left the country on business. I needed answers. I needed to understand the process better. So, to make sure that nothing got lost in translation, I drove one and a half hours (in terrible traffic) to the Thai Embassy to speak with the Consul. He phoned the Thailand Department of Social Welfare office and asked the many questions that James and I had. The information he gleaned helped clarify some things; however, it did not mean the process would happen any quicker than before. My eyes watered several times, but the tears did not spill over. The Consul had said that he admired us because so many people would have given up by then. He said that if we became discouraged then we needed to visit him more often so that he could encourage us not to give up. He also said that he liked being a mediator for us because it gave him an opportunity to practice his English.

A couple of days later, my friend Teri replied, "Hang in there, Sister! I'm sorry this is such an agonizing process, and part of me says 'I'm sorry I got you into this' but the other part still sees the hand of God in it from the beginning. I pray He gives you all you need to make it to the next step and to follow patiently to the end—whatever that may be."

God loves to bless his children! That very weekend at church the pastor shared from several verses, but one really stood out to me: Hebrews 5:8—*"Though a Son, He learned obedience through what He suffered."* I prayed that I would also learn obedience to the Father through my trials. Over the following days, my Bible reading through the Psalms brought me to Psalm 30 and 31. These words reminded me that weeping is okay, but need not continue! Psalm 31 also reminded me that God knows me! He knows the times my eyes have been worn out. He knows my "years of groaning" in this regard. He leads and guides me for HIS Name's sake. His great goodness is stored up for me. He hears the sound of my pleading. He wonderfully shows me His faithful love!

Looking out our bedroom window, I prayed to this end—that God would show me His love, His presence. At that very moment, more than twenty-five bright green parrots descended and landed in the two trees across the street. I know because I counted them! Goose bumps crawled up my arms as God's love and joy flooded my soul at the beauty of His creation right there in the midst of the physical and emotional desert in which I found myself.

The next committee matching date, June 14, 2006, came with no news. Rachel and I had been meeting weekly over the past year sharing our hearts. "How long will this take?" I exclaimed. The labor pains seemed so intense. God faithfully opened this door; I could not stop believing at this point that He would bring it to pass. After our prayer time,

I went home and poured out my thoughts in a song with this repeating refrain:

> *Like those who've gone before me,*
> *Lord, teach me how to say:*
> *Lead and I will follow, wherever you will go*
> *In the hours of darkness*
> *and through the raging storm*
> *As long as you are with me, I'll never be alone*
> *Jesus, God Almighty….*
> *Lead me home.*
> *--Delana2006*

On July 31st James called Ana. I suppose we thought maybe he could get a different result. Or perhaps I had grown weary of receiving the disappointing news. She told him that we had not yet received a profile because we had three children. "What does that have to do with it?" our middle son questioned—frustratingly voicing what was on our hearts. She did say that she would send us an e-mail with more information the next day. That e-mail did not come.

Perhaps James wanted to offer me a diversion. Whatever the reason, he encouraged me to go back to school and complete the education degree I had been working on when we got married. After considering my options, I enrolled in Liberty University's distance learning program that fall. They accepted all of my previous hours and gave me credit for work and life experiences that I documented through their portfolio course. That fall, I took the portfolio development course and began working on portfolios to submit for credit. Later on, I would take one eight-week course at a time and inch closer towards completing my degree.

Also in September I had scheduled an October/November trip to Thailand for a training meeting of education consultants. I called Ana to confirm that she would be in her office during that time so that I could come for a visit. At the conclusion of my training, I traveled by *tuk-tuk* (a Thai three-wheeled motorized vehicle) to the first location for which I had an address—a hospital. At the hospital, I struggled to find someone who spoke English so that I could find out how to get to the Thai Department of Social Services.

On November 2, I sat down across the desk from Ana for the first time. After small talk, she brought out a rather large bound ledger with information on waiting children. I reminded her that we had been waiting a very long time to receive our first referral. She went down the list saying, "Boy, boy, boy, boy, girl . . ." and then looked to see if the age and special need matched our case.

She came up with three possibilities that day: (1) a seven-year-old girl with one arm shorter than the other and some missing fingers, (2) a five-year-old girl with an artificial right eye and (3) a three-year-old girl with hearing loss in one ear due to ear infections. She would not give me any more information on the three girls at that time. She asked me to talk with my husband and decide if we wanted to move forward with one of these.

I phoned James in the Middle East and let him know how the visit went. In his mind, only one option seemed to fit our family. The first one was older than we had hoped, and we thought she would have difficulty adjusting to a new language and culture. James thought the youngest would have difficulty learning English due to her hearing loss, and he knew that the age gap between her and our boys would be even greater. That left the five-year-old girl. "Call Ana before you return home and see if she can give you additional information now," James responded.

The next day I called Ana from the guest house and asked her if she could send more information on the five-year-old girl. "I will fax it to the guest house where you are staying," she replied. No fax arrived; I left for home two days later.

A month passed, and we began once again to decorate our home for Christmas. With temperatures still reaching 100°F during the day, it did not feel like Christmastime. Nevertheless, we decorated and placed our little tree in one corner of the living-room. On an opposite wall, we hung stockings. There would be no snow and no extended family, but dear friends would be coming to visit.

Korean-Canadian friends we made in Central Asia came to spend the holidays with us. We visited museums and a petting zoo. Their three children were a little bit younger than ours. We exchanged gifts and enjoyed watching the kids play together, as they had done in Central Asia many years before. They stayed long enough to ring in the new year with us. We all prayed together regarding the adoption process, and they helped us keep our focus on the Lord.

We could not believe that Ana had not sent any details yet. All we knew about the little girl was that she was five years old and had an artificial eye.

I cried out to God and spilled my thoughts onto the pages of my journal . . .

IN THE UNSEEN

I am no warrior.
I can't sit and wait day in and day out
For nothing.
You are so silent!
Please, God, speak! Say something!
Crash like Thunder!
Do something.
Move this mountain…
This mountain that is falling on me,
Crushing me,
Suffocating me.
I need a light at the tunnel's end.
You are Light.
Send Your Light.
Show your light to me.
Why should I keep hoping?
Believing?
Why shouldn't I give up?
Because
Somewhere in my heart
Where the Spirit dwells
I still believe in
Miracles.
--Delana2006

Finally, Friday December 8, 2006, Ana sent the following e-mail:

> *"I would like to send you some information of Miss Luke-Mai. She was born on February 2, 2001. When she was born, she weighed less than five pounds. Moreover, the doctor diagnosed that she was iron deficient, had Retinoblastoma and enucleation of her right eye. Then the doctor operated her right eye. Presently, she wears an artificial eye. I attached the medical letter for your consideration.*
>
> *I had told you that she stayed in Home for Girls, however, last week I visited her, and I was surprised that she moved again to Home for Mentally Disabled Babies. However, she is a healthy child, usually she is a cheerful girl, but sometimes she will be upset and cry without any reason. Yesterday, I talked to a social worker at the Babies' Home, who said that Luke-Mai just moved to her home so she does not know her information so much. However, she will send the updated information of Luke-Mai to me in the next week. And I will forward the information to you. Best, Ana."*

Retino-*what?* James and I immediately searched the Internet for answers. We soon discovered that Retinoblastoma meant cancer on the retina. Two forms existed, the genetic form and the non-genetic form. It seemed from our research that the genetic form had a 90% recurrence of cancer either in the other eye or some other part of the body. James could not imagine what would happen to me if we adopted this little girl, only to lose her to cancer a year or two later. Feeling that I would certainly go insane he said, "I think we better at least find out which form of Retinoblastoma she had. And, if she had the genetic type, we should really think about making another choice."

We immediately wrote Ana with our questions. Unfortunately, she had gone on maternity leave and did not reply. Eventually, Ana's director Sadie took over our case. A month later, January 17, 2007, we learned that they did not know which form of Retinoblastoma the little girl had and that the tests to find out cost more than they wanted to pay. During that time we began writing family, friends, doctors, eye surgeon friends and many others asking for prayer and information. Many e-mails began flooding my inbox. We took great interest in an e-mail from my twin sister. She had written one of her husband's relatives, Melissa, who wrote a long letter with details about having Retinoblastoma. Here are some excerpts from her letter:

> *"The most important thing I think is not if the little girl is right for her, but is she right for the little girl. If this young girl does develop issues along the way she will need someone extremely strong to hold her hand. Not everyone is up for this, especially if it is a choice. My disease has brought me a lot of heartache and fear. It has also blessed me with a very strong bond within my family and amazing inner strength. I can't imagine having this type of relationship with my family if it wasn't for the obstacles that we have overcome together . . . and of course with God's help. If this is the little girl that your sister is suppose to have, I am sure that she will not waiver on her decision regardless of the health issue. It is hard to know that the little girl had Retinoblastoma. Unfortunately, there is no way to know what will happen. My father gave me some great advice when I was diagnosed with*

my disease. He said, 'You can worry about this every day of your life and live in turmoil, or you can worry about this when you have to, and then live every other day like it doesn't exist.' I of course decided that option two was the best choice.

I still believe this to this day. If it isn't one thing it will probably be something else. We all have our issues. Sometimes, believe it or not, I thank God for the disease that I inherited. When I look around I feel pretty lucky. I am sure most people would not want to trade places with me; the funny thing is that there are not too many people that I would trade places with. It gives me a different outlook on life, and it has helped me more than it has ever hurt me."

Of all the things Melissa had said, the thing that stood out most was to stop asking if this little girl was the right girl for our family and start asking if we could be the right family for this little girl. This totally changed the way we looked at the decision we needed to make. Could we be the right family for the needs she faced? Could we trust God to see us through the difficult times? We had prayed for two years that the first referral would be the child God had for us. Would we have the faith to believe it now?

Before writing Sadie at the Welfare Department on February 8, 2007, we wrote Melissa first:

"We reached a crisis of belief. God pierced our hearts; we had to ask ourselves if we would trust Him or signs and science. We know that His word says that faith that requires sight is not faith at all. We decided to send the acceptance letter stating that we would accept Luke-Mai

regardless of the outcome of the testing. So, our action was our decision to trust Him completely. If He believes that we would be the right family for Luke-Mai, then we trust that the matching committee will accept this match. We have put the situation back into His hands, where it belongs, and we have peace. Not just me and James, but all three of our boys also have peace that this is right." Valentine's Day came and one of the most special Valentine's of all—an e-mail from Sadie with a picture of the little girl and more information. In addition to height, weight, development and background, we learned a little about her personality from Sadie, who shared that this little girl was "quite short-tempered, hyperactive, and has a short period of time of concentration and speech delayed development." Sweet and spicy! From that moment, I began to carry her picture in a silver heart locket that James had bought for me. And, we began to refer to her as Jade.

The Adoption Review Board met on February 27, 2007, and approved us to adopt Jade. We did not waste any time telling our family and friends and making plans. We would travel to Thailand one month later. Thankfully, the boys had a youth retreat to attend for part of the three weeks that we would be away. The rest of the time they would stay with close friends. We worked tirelessly obtaining her tourist visa, sending pictures of our house and family to her, purchasing airline tickets and preparing our hearts and home.

Not living in America or Thailand meant that we not only had to fulfill the U.S. entry requirements, but we also had to obtain a visa for Jade to enter the U.A.E. Other expatriates were also adopting children abroad, yet the concept of adoption remained rather unfamiliar to immigration authorities. At one point we thought we would never be granted a visa for Jade to enter the country.

Once again James and I found ourselves in the immigration office being passed from one person to another, no one taking the time to truly understand our situation and what it was that we needed. After being denied a visa four times, we stood out in the hallway frustrated, wondering what we were going to do. A man who frequently visited the immigration office for the purpose of obtaining visit visas overheard us talking and invited us to come to his place of business to explain our situation to him. He was a person of peace that God had sent to help us in our time of need. His fluency in both Arabic and English—plus his familiarity with the visa process and immigration officers—allowed him to easily obtain the visa we needed on the paperwork we filled out.

The documents the welfare department sent to us contained information regarding Jade's biological family. Her birth mother had abandoned her at the hospital in need of cancer treatment in 2002. It was not until 2004 that the welfare department located Jade's birth mother and gave her an opportunity to have her daughter back. This woman had never married Jade's biological father, and she had lost contact with him. As a single mother, she had two more children for whom she struggled to provide. Jade's biological father could not be found. The birth mother terminated her rights in July 2004, at which point Jade became adoptable.

Upon leaving the hospital, Jade spent three and a half years in a baby home, followed by six months in the orphan home for school-aged girls. Because of her developmental delays, she could not cope with beginning school and living with age-mates. Her speech and language skills lagged her peers by three years. Not having any other solution for her social workers transferred her to the special needs home. Five months after she arrived in the special needs orphanage we would be bringing her home.

James and I thought that Jade being an older orphan might have attachment issues. We thought that growing up in an orphanage run predominately by women might also cause her to be afraid of men. So we prayed that she would bond quickly to James.

Just like any expectant mother proudly shows sonogram pictures, I showed numerous people the few photos we had of Jade. In the silver heart locket that James had given me, I carried a photo of Jade on one side and the phrase "God has heard" on the other. I thought the announcement of our approved match would put me on cloud nine, but it did not. I thought having her picture and showing it to others would make me glow with excitement, but it did not. Perhaps my heart feared something would go wrong. "Maybe," I thought, "it will not feel real until the day we meet her."

Around the middle of March we had received an e-mail from Thai Social Services. Sadie had tried to prepare us for what to expect:

> *"Take your first day to rest from your journey. On Thursday March 29th take a taxi to my office. Ana or I will take you out to the home for special needs' children. The first day you will spend a couple of hours getting to know Luke-Mai and allowing her to become familiar with you. The next day you may take her out for a few hours, but she will sleep at the orphanage. On the third or later visit, you may take her back to your accommodation until the final hearing. Towards the end of your stay, you*

*will bring her to meet before the Adoption Review
Board for final approval."*

We thought this sounded like good advice. It would
allow us a few days to take care of some business before
having our little girl around every moment of the day. We
needed to take care of completing her visa to return with us
to the Middle East, and we also needed to visit the American
Embassy.

March 27th arrived and we loaded our bags into the car
to head to the airport, anticipating what the next few days
would hold. Friends of ours had made a recording for us of
many Thai phrases for us to learn. We learned toddler food
and bathroom terminology and words of comfort like: "It's
okay. Don't cry. I love you." The long flight to Thailand
allowed me plenty of time to continue studying these phrases
and to contemplate what the days ahead had in store for us.
This pregnancy had lasted nine long years, and the flight to
Thailand became my drive to the hospital to deliver.

8. Delivery

"For his anger lasts only a moment, but his favor lasts a lifetime; weeping may remain for a night, but rejoicing comes in the morning." -- Psalm 30:5 NIV

On Thursday, Ana took us out to the orphanage. During the 30-45 minute drive, she reiterated what Sadie had told us would occur. I began practicing the Thai phrases I knew with Ana during the ride.

The orphanage resembled a small village within the outskirts of the city. Many buildings and homes occupied the compound grounds. Ana, James and I walked past the director's office and into a small air-conditioned office in the bottom of a large two- to three-story building; the rest of that building did not have air conditioning.

A lady in the office seated us at a long table opposite several desks, some that had computers on them. A package of markers and sheets of plain white paper lay on the table. Someone else brought us juice and water while we waited a few more minutes.

"Look, I see her coming!" exclaimed James. She wore an orange-yellow, cottony dress with a spring-green sash. We both stood and watched our daughter descend the stairs; she held tightly to her teacher's hand. *Our daughter.* That phrase still sounded unreal; no fireworks going off in my head and no hallelujah chorus resounding in my ears. Butterflies in my stomach better described the way I felt at that moment.

Her teacher, Ahmie, greeted us in Thai, since she did not speak English. She turned and said something to Jade, who hid behind her and peeked out at us shyly. This tiny girl, who had just turned six nearly two months before, looked more like a three year old. Soon she warmed up to the office staff and office area—an environment she had obviously become very familiar with over the past four months living in this special needs orphanage. She went over to Tom, one of the office workers, and sat on his lap while he flipped through pictures on his computer. She appeared very fascinated and familiar with the computer, taking the mouse from Tom and exploring on her own.

James and I engaged the other staff in signing their names and messages for Jade on a large pink pillowcase. I had read various stories of adoptive parents having their child's friends and workers in an orphanage sign journals, T-shirts, and blankets. I had also read about parents who used a pillowcase that they took from home to provide consistency and comfort to their child while at the orphanage, at the hotel and later back home. So, I combined the two ideas.

Before long, Jade joined us at the table where she, Ahmie and I drew pictures with the markers. Ana translated to us what Ahmie told Jade, "See this house? See this person? This is my house. This is me. I am waving to you. You are on an airplane. You are going with your mommy and daddy to your new home."

Someone may have prompted her in Thai, I do not know, but suddenly Jade latched onto James' hand and led him out to the playground with me tagging along. God had answered our prayers for her to bond with James. We spent time with Jade on the playground swinging together. James helped her take pictures with our digital camera, and she fully enjoyed seeing the images appear on the digital display. Next, she showed us around to other buildings on the grounds that provided housing, instruction and care for around 1000 children. Before long, she reached up her arms wanting James to carry her, which he gladly did. Finally, Ana joined us and led us to the infirmary so we could learn how to care for Jade's prosthetic eye.

While we waited for one of the nurses to come, we had the opportunity to observe the baby room, a long room lined with rows of cribs—at least one hundred. Each crib contained two babies lying feet to feet. On that day, three college-aged students had come to volunteer their time. They played keyboard, flute and guitar, and they sang praise songs for the babies. Then, they went around and spent time holding and loving on each of the children. They must have known the developmental necessity of their affection, time and music. What a precious gift to give these tiny ones! Just outside the door of the infirmary, we noticed children being brought in—some on stretchers, some carried in arms. Most of the children at this special needs orphanage had mental or physical handicaps of one sort or another.

The nurse arrived, which caused Jade to immediately begin to tremble. She knew that something she did not like would soon occur. Without too much difficulty, the nurse took out Jade's artificial eye and began to clean it. While she cleaned it, Ana translated some basic instructions for us regarding the care of a prosthetic eye. When the artificial eye lay in the nurse's hand, I noticed that it more closely resembled a very thick and large contact lens rather than a marble. The real battle began when the nurse attempted to return the plastic eye to Jade's eye socket. Jade squeezed her eyes shut, twisted and turned her body, screamed and cried while the nurse and several others held her down and forced the eye back. No wonder she hated the infirmary! There has to be a better way to do this, I thought. I wondered if I would ever be able to perform that task. [Much later we learned that the eye had been polished to a sharp edge, causing pain and bleeding. When we got her a new prosthetic, she could easily take it out and put it back in by herself.]

Ahmie had joined us at the infirmary to help the nurses. During the past hour of visiting, we learned that Jade had not grown up with her birth name but with the nickname Luke-Mai, which means Lace. I wondered if she received that name during her surgery and operation due to her fragile condition. Did a nurse or doctor begin calling her that? We can only imagine how frail she must have been during infancy while undergoing chemotherapy that lasted more than 6 months. We later learned from her medical records that she was in and out of the hospital for over a year with pneumonia, bronchitis, chicken pox and a host of other illnesses due to her fragile condition after the chemotherapy. Thankfully, we did not spend a long time in the infirmary, which did not produce happy thoughts for any of us.

Next we went to Ahmie's house—a narrow, two-story home on the compound. Once again, Ana translated Ahmie's words to us, "For the past six weeks Luke-Mai has lived here in my home. She came to us with a very strong will, and I needed to work with her daily and hourly. The director and teachers also felt that she needed to learn how to live in a real house, rather than in a room full of children."

As we approached Ahmie's home, a boy and two dogs joined us. The small, cheerful boy had recently turned twelve, and Ahmie had taken him in and treated him like a son. Matt obviously had mental and developmental challenges, but he did not lack for smiles and compassion. He rode up on his bicycle with a package of chewing gum and a drink for Jade. He obviously cared very much about her. Before entering the house, Jade bent over, loved on the dogs and allowed them to return the affection with kisses all over her face. Yes! She and our black lab would get along fabulously!

A bed occupied the space just inside the front door, on the left. Pink and blue sheets, teddy bears and Winnie-the-Pooh neatly decorated the top of it. "Does Jade sleep here?" I asked.

"No, she sleeps upstairs," Ana translated as Ahmie explained that someone was currently sleeping upstairs, and we could not go up. I wondered if she gave us the real reason that we could not go up, or if she just did not want us to see what the upstairs looked like.

Jade continued to proudly show us around the tiny but clean downstairs. A small kitchen and bathroom lay on the other side of the wall from the room we entered. The bathroom contained a sink, a shower sprayer and a squatty potty—an Asian toilet that was a ceramic hole in the ground with a place to stand. The kitchen consisted of a free-standing metal sink with a water spigot and a one-burner stove. Baskets held dry goods and dishes. That was all of the downstairs.

Ahmie handed us a small plastic bag containing all of Jade's earthly possessions: a hand-sewn flowery shower wrap made from a towel, one pull-up for nighttime, two shirts, two shorts, two dresses, a pair of socks, two pairs of underwear, a stuffed doll and the photo album we had sent ahead of time. Other than that, her only other items included the dress she wore and the jingly flip-flops on her feet. Tears came to James' eyes when he reflected on the life Jade had been living; it struck him that everything she owned as a six-year-old girl we now carried away in a small plastic grocery bag.

From Ahmie's house we headed to the director's office where we finally met the director of the special needs orphanage. She was a very kind and hospitable Thai woman in her 50s. More people signed Jade's pillowcase; we took many pictures and exchanged gifts with the director. The director gave us some handmade Thai vases and presented us with an album of Jade that the workers had put together. Tom, the office worker with whom Jade seemed to enjoy spending time, also presented us with a CD containing many photos as well.

"I called a taxi for you; it is on its way," said Ana.

"Oh, thank you! When can we come back for our next visit?" I asked.

"You can take her with you now," she replied.

"Great!" I thought, thinking they must have decided to let us have our first outing today. "When do we need to bring her back?"

"We want you to keep her until the hearing with the Adoption Review Board," she said.

Shocked, confused and totally taken by surprise describes my next emotions (and likely the look on my face). Why had they changed the plan? Did they want us to have additional time to bond? Or, perhaps, they wanted to make sure we would have enough time to see if we still felt the same way about her after spending more time together.

When the taxi pulled up, we exchanged hugs with several of the workers. James took Jade by the hand and started to put her into the vehicle. She screamed and tried to keep herself outside of the car. I climbed in first, and James continued to try and hand Jade to me. Unsuccessful, he held her tightly against himself and crawled into the taxi beside me, with her flailing and screaming. Any child would have responded in the same way.

My heart ached for what she must have been feeling. The workers knew, and we knew, what Jade's life would be like if no one adopted her, if she was left to be raised in a special needs orphanage. Even though workers had spent several weeks preparing Jade for this moment, nothing could prepare a child for saying good-bye to everything familiar and leaving what had become home to live with total strangers. My mind drifted to my sons when they were six years old, thinking about what it would have been like for them to go through this experience.

Ana decided to get into the front seat of the taxi and spoke calmly to Jade in Thai. Good! I thought Ana would ride back to the guest house with us. Jade's screams turned to crying quietly and then a few sniffles. One block from the orphanage, Ana jumped out at the stop sign. Hmmm. I guess we are on our own now. Jade watched out the window as we headed to the guest house where we were staying. Her crying ceased while she took in many sites along the way: fruit and vegetable vendors on the sides of the road; motorcycles zooming in and out and around the traffic, sometimes with a father, mother and two or three children squeezed in between them; *Tuk-tuks* carrying passengers around to various markets and tourist destinations; and little red pick-up trucks lined with benches in the back for transporting larger groups of people.

About forty-five minutes later, we arrived at our accommodation. The guest house buildings, situated like a motel with outside entrances to the bedrooms, surrounded a courtyard with a playground. Jade cheered up immediately and joined other children playing on the playground. I sat back and observed everything going on around me.

Everything seemed like a movie rather than reality. It reminded me of lying in the hospital bed, medicated from having my tubes tied, watching people come and go from the room after giving birth to my third son. In that sleepy stage I did not even remember my grandmother calling to congratulate me.

That was *my daughter* playing on the playground. Would I even remember that moment in the days to come?

James and Jade on Jade's first visit back to Thailand January 2011.

Jade giving roses to Delana's paternal grandmother the day after her grandfather died, summer 2008.

Jade in our living room three months after bringing her home, July 2007.

Jade helping Delana blow out her birthday candles on July 4, 2007.

Jade in a toy store in Dubai summer 2007.

December 2007—Our first Christmas together.

Jade swinging in Bulverde, Texas, summer 2008.

Summer 2010 looking out on the Arabian Gulf.

Stewart family Christmas 2010, f-Jordan, Jade, Josh; b-Delana, James, Jake.

Jade and cousin Rylee at big brother Josh's wedding summer 2011. Jade was a fairy-princess flower girl.

9. Newborn

Religion that God our Father accepts as pure and faultless is this: to look after orphans and widows in their distress and to keep oneself from being polluted by the world. —James 1:27 NIV

Thankfully, most of the guest house staff spoke Thai and engaged Jade in friendly chit-chat. After some time of playing, we went on a walk to the nearest shopping center, about a mile away. Jade held James' hand and jingle-jingle went her flip-flops as we walked down the road. Because of the heat, we stopped by a corner store and bought some drinks and a small bag of crushed ice. Jade loved carrying her bag of ice and eating it all the way to the store.

Our first order of business was to buy clothes. We had not brought any with us, not knowing what sizes she would need. We had originally thought that we could buy some things for her during our initial visits and outings. Now we needed everything right away: night clothes, under clothes, swim wear, socks and shoes. While shopping for clothes, Jade's appreciation for small things amazed James. He later wrote a friend the following:

> *"As children, we were never thrilled about getting new clothes for a present, those were just basic necessities that we expected. Not so with Jade: every pair of socks, every pair of panties, cheap sunglasses, tennis shoes and new outfits were all received with great jubilation.*

> *She was so proud of her new tennis shoes that we could hardly take them off her feet for the first three days. I hope she will continue to be thankful for all God is blessing her with. Perhaps I can learn from her to appreciate even the simple and common things in life like a toothbrush, a comb, socks and a pillow."*

We ate pepperoni pizza for lunch and ice cream sundaes for dessert; Jade seemed to enjoy both (though James had to finish her ice cream). On the long walk back, James picked her up and carried her part of the way. Evening had come, and we returned to our room at the guest house. We showed Jade pictures of her brothers in her special album that she had received a month before we arrived, and we then presented her with gifts from each of them. Each brother had made her a card out of his favorite color of construction paper with a picture of himself inside. All three had chosen items for Jade's hair, also in their favorite colors: orange, green and blue. In addition to their gifts, we had brought play dough and a few small toys.

Soon bedtime came and with it a demonstration of Jade's strong will. A few weeks prior to traveling to Thailand, I had sent an e-mail to Teri's friend who fostered Thai babies and young children. I wanted to know how and when to address discipline issues. No stranger to the need for firm but loving discipline from bringing up three boys, I still felt nervous about this issue regarding adopting an older child. Claire graciously responded the very next day:

> *"The sooner you start the better! A lot of adopted families are scared to discipline at first but that makes it hard for you and the child later. At first the child receives a lot of gifts, candy, cookies and ice cream. The adoptive parents feel sorry for them*

for being without a family; then all of a sudden the parents decide to stop some behaviors of the child. The child becomes confused, 'Why should I stop now? I have acted like this from the time they met me.'

I have seen the adopted family buy the child something at every store they entered. So the child thinks 'Wow! I always get to buy whatever I want;' then this comes to a stop, and the child thinks 'but why and what did I do wrong this time?'

When you discipline, you must make sure the child understands. I saw this with a family that was adopting an older child that knew some English. The child only knew enough English to make matters worse for him. The family thought that he understood more than he did, and they assumed too much. He was always getting into trouble because they would say 'Now I know he knew what I was talking about and still did it anyway.'

So I think your biggest problem will be communication: you need to make sure that you communicate when disciplining or before disciplining because you may have thought she knew what you were saying. When you ask her if she understands she will shake her head yes, but really she did not understand."

I decided right then that I would do the difficult thing and begin loving but firm discipline from the beginning. But this was *day one!* "Do you think she meant day one?" I wondered to myself. Jade did not struggle with brushing teeth and changing into pajamas, but I could see that she had not planned on spending the night with us.

Our upstairs motel room had three beds: one king size and two twins. With a few Thai phrases and hand signals, I showed Jade that Daddy and I would sleep in the big bed, and she could choose one of the two twin beds. She shook her head no. Not wanting a battle our first night, I pushed the two twin beds together and again in Thai and hand signals explained that she could have the big bed and Daddy and I would sleep in the two twin beds.

"No!" she exclaimed in Thai, throwing herself down on the bed while bursting into tears. Did she want to sleep in bed with us? Did she not want to be here at all? Either one would certainly make sense. James and I both tried to hold her and console her. She made a break for the door and quickly figured out how to unlock it. She tried to make a run for it. While James pulled her away from the door, I discovered an additional lock up at the very top of the door, a way to deadbolt it out of her reach. She kept her eyes glued on me while I locked that bolt. Realizing that she could not leave, she threw herself down on the floor by the bathroom door and beat her head against the wall. First I tried to hold her, and then James tried, to keep her from clawing herself with her hands, digging her heels into her legs and banging her head on the floor and wall.

Pulling away from James, she grabbed her doll and crawled under the king-sized bed and sobbed. The crying eventually stopped and occasional, tearful, short breaths replaced it. As soon as it had become evident that she had fallen asleep, we gently pulled her out and placed her in the king-sized bed. Within five minutes, she grabbed her pillow and doll and lay down on the floor between the bed and bathroom. We covered her up and let her be.

James and I then prepared for bed, but could not get to sleep. After an emotional first day, all I could do was lean my head on James' shoulder and cry. "Are we doing the right thing?" I asked. Even though for several weeks workers had explained to Jade what would take place, she must have felt like we had kidnapped her, holding her against her will in a locked room.

The fireworks had come, just not the ones I had anticipated. When would I be overjoyed that after nine years of pregnancy and a year of labor God had finally answered my prayer? How long would it take Jade to accept me like a mother? She seemed to readily accept James at first, but she did not take to me initially. And, that first night she did not desire to bond with either one of us. Jade and I both cried ourselves to sleep that night.

In the morning, Jade awoke cheerful and ready to greet the day. She laughed as I attempted to open the door to head outside. I unlocked the handle and turned and pulled. Nothing! We were locked in, or so I thought. Jade giggled some more and then pointed to the deadbolt up at the top. She remembered the extra bolt. I had forgotten. I knew right then that we had a very clever, extremely observant daughter.

That day we took her to Ocean World where she got to see mermaids swim in the tanks with fish, shark and rays. She especially liked playing in the ball pit and tunnel section inside the aquarium. The mall in general fascinated Jade. She loved the mannequins and riding the escalators up and down—as good as any amusement park ride! She enjoyed Chicken McNuggets at McDonalds for lunch and saw many things that day that tickled and delighted her.

We filled the week with lots of activity. We tried to stay out and about most of the time. Jade loved riding the sky train. *Tuk-tuks* scared her though, and she did not want to ride them. Since they were the cheapest form of transportation, we eventually convinced her to ride on one. Her fear of them made me wonder if she had seen or been involved in a *Tuk-Tuk* accident.

Some days we hung out at the guest house and let her splash in a kiddie-pool, which she thoroughly enjoyed. Very brave about going under water, she held her breath, splashed, flipped and dove right into the little pool. James played on the playground with her, running through the fort and across the bridge. He has always loved teasing and quickly learned that Jade did, too. It seemed like they were partners in crime—meant for each other.

By the fourth day, things smoothed out some, and we wrote our friends to let them know how things were going:

> *"This is our fourth day with Jade. We still can't believe they let us have her the very first day! We were surprised! She is full of energy. She is very active and loves to ride the bicycle here and play basketball. She is learning so quickly . . . it amazes me. She has some discipline issues . . . and some daily fits . . . but these are getting easier to deal with, and she stops crying sooner now. She has learned to say 'I love you,' 'hello,' 'goodbye,' 'please,' and 'thank you' . . ."*

Once while taking an almost daily walk to the nearby shopping center, something interesting happened. We had started a routine of her walking to the store and James carrying her on the way back. This particular day she wanted to be carried on the way to the store as well. "No!" she yelled, firmly planting her bottom on the ground and not budging.

One of us disciplined her and told her in Thai to walk. She got the idea that we were not giving in to her strong will. Halfway there, she stopped. She stared off in the distance and did not respond to our attempts to get her attention. She then began to roll her eyes, kind of like having a type of seizure. Thankfully, we quickly realized that our daughter did not really have seizures but had learned very well at the special needs orphanage how to imitate those who really did have seizures. We began understanding right then some of her manipulation and other survival skills.

Jade showed us another side of her personality, one of compassion and empathy for others. Like me, James also sent an e-mail to a friend during our first week with Jade:

> *"We have had Jade now for six days. She attached to me first and then to Delana after 24 hours. Those first 24 hours were really hard for Delana, but now that Jade has learned 'Mommy,' everything is fine. She has a temper and throws a couple of fits each day when she does not get her way; but after she settles down, she forgets about it. She is learning to obey, something she is not used to.*
>
> *On one of our trips to the shopping center, Jade and I roamed around the store while Delana shopped for some clothes. Jade spotted a little pink purse on a clearance shelf. She started asking me for the purse, so I handed it to her to hold. I could tell she really liked it, and the price was only 30 U.S. cents, so I bought it for her.*
>
> *This became her favorite new possession; she even wanted to sleep with it. The next day, I dropped a one baht coin (worth about three U.S. cents) in the purse and let her discover it while she played. She*

was so excited that I had put a coin in the purse. She did not want Delana or me to touch it. The next day we were with the social worker who told me that Jade could buy a piece of candy with one baht, and that is why she loved it so much.

Delana gave Jade a second one baht coin to carry around in her purse. She counted the coins everywhere we went. One day she lost one of the coins in the blanket on the bed at the guest house. They had to search for awhile until they found it.

Two days later we were in a store where there was a Red Cross collection box by the register. Jade looked at the box, then looked at her purse and seemed deep in thought for a few moments. Then she reached in her purse and dropped one of the coins in the box with a big smile on her face. We were amazed that she so happily gave up one of her precious coins.

The next day, while walking in an outdoor bazaar, we saw a young blind man singing. He had a wooden box for collections. Jade watched him for a few moments with her only eye and then tapped me on the shoulder to take her to the blind man. I walked over, and she pulled out her one remaining coin and dropped it in the box. She grinned from ear to ear, and giggled excitedly.

I was so touched that Jade gave up both coins to someone needier, rather than buying candy. It reminded me of the widow in the Gospel story that gave her last two coins in the offering. You can only imagine just how proud I was of her. I am so

> *encouraged by this sign that God is at work in Jade's heart, and it is quite convicting that one who has so little is so cheerful and enthusiastic about giving."*

We would later learn just how compassionate and empathetic she felt towards those with disabilities or other needs.

At the end of our first week in Thailand, we met with the Adoption Review Board. Ana had told us to dress business-like for the meeting with the Board, but assured us this final stage was only a formality. Along with many other adoptive parents and children, we waited for our turn to appear before the Board. While waiting, we visited with a mom we had met in Ana's office earlier in the week. Her one-year-old son seemed calmer this time. Before, both mom and child were noticeably rattled. She had told us then, "He just won't stop crying. I've been up all night!" I had assured her that it would just take time. The day of the big meeting, he held onto her tightly and at that moment was not crying.

Our time to meet the Board arrived. Pleasant smiles of men and women my parents' age greeted us. They asked us many questions, some of which we had previously answered on the application or by e-mail. They wanted to know about our boys, our discipline practices/beliefs and our plans for educating Jade. They knew that I homeschooled the boys, a new concept for them. We assured them that we would do whatever Jade needed in terms of schooling. We knew that at first she mostly needed to learn English and learn to love and be loved by our family. Towards the end of our 20-minute session, the director of the Board turned to Jade and in Thai asked her, "Do you want to go with this family?"

How would she answer that? Less than a week ago she screamed getting into the taxi. She experienced our love and affection, but also experienced discipline. Would she tell them that she did not want to leave? Thankfully, she peeked up from her seated position on Daddy's lap and told them that she wanted to stay with us. They told us that she said that she loved us and wanted to go with us and was not afraid. Whew!

During our final week in Thailand, we needed to do several major things: take Jade to the doctor for a check-up, pick up Jade's entry visa, have all of her official Thai documents translated into English and purchase her ticket home. The doctor visit went well. An ophthalmologist checked her eyes and explained in a better way how to take the prosthetic eye out and put it back. A sweet pediatrician, Dr. Dane, gently checked Jade over and patiently answered our many medical questions. She set us at ease and expressed delight about our decision to adopt.

While we sat in the embassy office waiting for Jade's travel documents to be approved, Jade and I drew pictures. I drew a picture of an airplane. Then, I drew pictures of little houses and little people waving—her teacher Ahmie and her friend Matt. I reminded Jade of what Ahmie had told her about waving to her from the ground. I put Jade and Daddy and me inside the airplane, smiling and waving. Jade quickly took the pencil from my hand. I thought perhaps that she might erase herself from the airplane. Instead, she erased Ahmie and Matt from the ground and put them on the airplane. So, she did want to go with us—she just wanted her friends to come along, too.

During a busy day of having documents translated, we took time out to have lunch in a park and feed the ducks that swam in the canals. While watching Jade toss bread into the water, we noticed that other critters besides ducks inhabited this park: monitor lizards. These reptiles resembled small alligators, and their presence in the park surprised us. Though these four-to-six feet long lizards scared me, local children ran around chasing them into the water.

Finally, we headed to Thai Airways to purchase her ticket. We were able to change our tickets and get the last few remaining seats on a flight leaving three days earlier than we had planned (and arriving in the afternoon instead of evening)! We were going home. *Home.* That meant she was coming with us. She would be our daughter. No stars were in my eyes, and no hallelujah chorus was ringing in my ears. But other emotions abounded! I felt relief. I felt thankful. I felt compassion for this small, adorable little girl.

It had been more than ten years since the dream—since conception. I had carried the desire and the concept of adopting a child for a really long time. I did not understand the strange sensation I felt. I could not explain it either, except for realizing that I had experienced carrying children in my womb, so perhaps it had something to do with pre-birth bonding. For James, there had been no pre-birth bonding experience with which to compare it. Jade had already wrapped herself tightly around his finger in less than three weeks' time. He hoisted her up onto his shoulders, and we strolled out of the Thai Airway ticketing office.

The only thing that remained for us to do in Thailand was to see some sights, call the boys and let them know of our earlier return and pack our bags.

Delana H. Stewart

RELIGHTING THE WICK

I thank You Lord
For making me, for hearing me
Drawing Yourself near to me
For renewing my strength
Relighting the wick
For bandaging my wounds
For comfort, protection, wisdom and hope
You are Holy, Awesome
Beyond comprehension
You are Mighty, Defender, Conqueror, King
You are Daddy, You are Lover, You are Friend!
--Delana2003

10. Homecoming

*Now we see but a poor reflection as in a mirror;
then we shall see face to face. Now I know in part;
then I shall know fully, even as I am fully known. I
Corinthians 13:12 NIV*

The night before we left Thailand, we checked our e-mail and sent a message to our sons. My friend Linda's timely letter brought much needed encouragement to get me through the difficult days to come:

> *"I know you want her to instantly love you the way you do her—it'll come. It will come! There are so many adjustments for all of you to make!*
>
> *I pray GRACE over each of you! It really touched my heart that she wanted James' hand to hold so much. Little girls love their daddies! I am sure that he offers her some safety and security which she has most likely desperately longed for.*
>
> *Sweet, sweet, sweet! I praise God for this gift of life and family he has given each of you."* After checking our luggage at the Thai Airways counter, we took a lot of pictures of Jade in scenic spots around the airport. She enjoyed watching planes take off and land while we waited for our departure time. Before long, James scooped up our little girl, and we boarded the plane for home.

Jade did very well on the airplane, which pleasantly surprised us. No fits! She absolutely enjoyed herself. The last hour she seemed a little restless, but she still did fabulously (who wouldn't be restless on a seven-hour flight). Before we had gone to Thailand, my prayer partner, Rachel, had brought two things for us to take to Jade: a teddy bear and a picture of her seven-year-old daughter hugging that bear. When we arrived at the airport, Rachel and her daughter had come to the airport with roses to greet us. Jade seemed truly happy to see a new friend she recognized from the photo.

When Jade saw her new brothers, she willingly let Jordan and then Jake carry her out of the airport and the rest of the way to the car. We had been looking at family pictures on the airplane; in the car on the way home, she pointed to pictures of her brothers and then pointed to each of them. She giggled a lot and teased the guys all the way home. Though she clung to Jordan and Jake at the airport, she quickly developed her strongest attachment to her oldest brother Josh.

Greeting our black lab Katy turned out to be a highlight of the day for Jade; the two became fast friends. Evening quickly approached, so we took Jade upstairs to let her see where everyone would sleep. At the top of the stairs we entered the common area, from which the three bedrooms connected. The master bedroom was on the right; Josh and Jake's room was straight ahead. We divided the long bedroom on the left with wardrobes and dressers for Jade and Jordan. An open area between the wall and first dresser allowed easy access inside the room. We showed Jade a mattress on our bedroom floor where she could come if she woke up in the middle of the night. Tired from the long trip, Jade quickly fell asleep. The big surprise came in the morning when I discovered her sleeping in big brother Jordan's bed. Evidently, even the older children must have shared beds at the orphanage. Once Jade learned to speak English, she let us know she always slept paired up with another child in her bed at different orphanages.

The days, weeks and months that followed seemed like a roller coaster. Jade's English improved rapidly. She enjoyed watching movies in both Thai and English. She enjoyed coloring and playing with the girls in our neighborhood. Those were definitely the high moments.

No one had prepared us for the difficulties we faced multiple times a day. At first the issues occurred mostly at bedtime. She did not want to go to bed before everyone else, and she did not want to sleep in her own bed. Before even arriving home, we had decided to fully follow the advice we had received. In addition to disciplinary advice, Claire told us to establish a routine from the beginning. She said to start out with what we expected to be the norm because it was always easier to make exceptions down the road. We would have loved to let her crawl in bed with us and snuggle her way to dreamland during the first weeks in her new home; however, we did not want that to be the norm; we did not want to begin that way and have her feel "unloved" when we changed the norm later. So, we always required that she start the evening in her own bed. We prayed with her, sang to her and played a cassette for her each night. We told her that if she woke up after Mommy had gone to sleep then she could come into our room and sleep on the mattress on the floor beside our bed.

Sounds good, right? She revolted! Each and every night for months she refused to stay in her bed. Almost every night she threw a fit about going to bed. But that was not all. Every day she would have three to five massive meltdowns—

tantrums of kicking, screaming, hitting and often times even hurting herself (usually scratching her arms and legs or banging her fists into her head). These occurred anytime she did not get her way—exactly. Many times I had to hold her with her back pressed against my chest and stomach, with my legs and arms separating her legs and arms to keep her from hurting herself during one of these meltdowns. She had more strength for her tiny size than any of my sons had at that age. She had definitely learned to be a fighter.

In moments when I did not have the strength to hold her during one of these meltdowns, I helped her into the shower and turned on the water. Initially, she did not like it, but it did the trick—the water caused her angry, hot, tense body to release. She would then crumple into my arms and let me hold her while she wept softly. I can understand how parents in a similar situation might find themselves tempted to flee or fight. They might leave their child alone, which would open up the opportunity for their child to truly endanger himself or herself; at the very least, an abandoned child would feel more abandoned. Other parents might find themselves shaking the child or otherwise abusing a child in this situation. A shower, on the other hand, provided a diversion for our daughter and allowed her hot temper to dissipate. It provided us with a safe way to stop her from endangering herself and a way to quickly bring her to a point of healing.

While raising and parenting three boys, James and I learned many parenting skills. For our sons, a time out in their room would be appropriate. For an abandoned child, time-outs needed to take place in the same room as the parents. Parenting a child with abandonment issues and attachment disorder was very different. We had never had a child that tried to hurt or endanger himself. We began to talk with counselors, pastors, friends and family, and we read many articles on the Internet concerning adopting older children. Through the years, we had read parenting books such as *The New Strong-Willed Child* by James Dobson and *Parenting with Love and Logic* by Cline and Fay. From Jed Baker's book *No More Meltdowns: Positive Strategies for Managing and Preventing Out-Of-Control Behavior,* we learned the importance of the crisis tool of distraction. I really do not recall how the idea of giving her a shower during a tantrum came to mind, but it worked great at keeping her from hurting herself. Thankfully, as she matured and developed reasoning skills and improved language skills, tantrums became few and far between.

To survive abandonment, cancer, chemotherapy and life in an orphanage, Jade had to be a fighter. Fighting had meant surviving. Upon entering a loving home, she had to learn how to give and receive love.

The social workers had told us Jade had a strong will, but somehow we never imagined that it would be so strong! Some well-meaning friends told me that I should just give her everything she wanted and have pity on her. I determined, instead, to do what was best for her—not necessarily what she wanted nor what would make life easier for me in the short-run. Like a horse whisperer who trains a wild filly, I somehow needed to find a way to understand and overcome Jade's fears, to gain her trust, to set boundaries and to convince her that she no longer had to fight her battles alone.

Thankfully, my eight-week college course for the spring semester got cancelled. I would not have been able to handle coursework on top of everything else. I wanted to work with Jade playing educational games similar to those I had used with my sons when they were young, but her strong will and lack of attention span caused every attempt to be futile.

One day during her first month home, Jade and I walked the dirt roads of our neighborhood. Just one street over, we passed a nursery/kindergarten. That day she heard children playing in the yard and kept saying, "Go there, Mama." So she and I went to check it out. She played with the children while I visited with the director. We decided to try it out the very next day for just one hour. I took a timer with us that I had been using at home. When Jade first joined our family, she did not want me out of her sight. She could not even handle my leaving the room for five minutes to check on the laundry.

I began to use a timer to help her see that Mommy would be back before that timer rang. Eventually, I lengthened time away from her to do tasks around the house. So, I took the timer to school that first day and set it for one hour. I made sure to show up in 45 minutes. Jade loved school and began going everyday from 8 a.m. to 1 p.m. This worked perfectly, allowing me the morning to help her brothers with their class work, answer work e-mails and clean the house. It also decreased the number of Jade's meltdowns I had to face each day. Unfortunately, it did not decrease the total number of meltdowns.

Jade attended that school for April, May and June of 2007, and the teacher allowed her to pretty much do her own thing, including roaming the halls and entering other classrooms. I know the teacher learned early on that it was the only way to have peace in the classroom, but it did not help Jade learn.

Towards the end of June a man from the Thai Embassy came to have our first post-placement home visit. We were a little nervous about how this visit would go. We had read of the importance of keeping up with an older adopted child's language and culture. We knew that typically children learn a new language better if they continue learning their mother tongue. Friends of ours who speak Thai fluently had tried to engage Jade in conversations in Thai, but she refused their attempts. For the first two months, she enjoyed watching cartoons and children's movies in Thai, but she quickly lost interest. While families should encourage language and culture, each adopted child will have different needs. Our six-year-old daughter had speech and developmental delays in her native language. She did not know colors, numbers or other words that a typical child her age would know.

The day of the post-placement visit, the man from the Thai Embassy tried to speak with Jade in Thai. She normally did not shy away from strangers, but she would not dialogue with him at all, until he began speaking to her in English. At that point we realized that she did not want to maintain a language she did not know or speak very well. In a few months her speaking abilities in English surpassed her speaking abilities in Thai, but her comprehension in English had not yet reached the level she had attained in Thai. In some ways, I wished we had made greater attempts to encourage her to continue to speak Thai, but with so many areas in which to help her we had to make some difficult choices. We did continue to expose her to Thai culture, holidays, foods and people. And we continue to hope that one day she will desire to learn Thai.

In July my parents came for a visit—they wanted to see their newest grandchild. She loved having grandparents doting on her and allowing her all kinds of treats and privileges. The day before they left to return to the U.S., Jade became very sad, mad even. When she understood that they would be leaving, she ran upstairs and slammed all the doors. Then, she got some of her favorite things and told me that she was going to go live with her friend (a neighbor two houses down). I knew how I would have handled this with my sons, but I felt unsure about how to handle it with an adopted child. I never wanted her to doubt our love and stability. I never wanted her to feel abandoned or unwanted. So I let her vent, then I followed her out the front door and to the doorstep of our neighbor.

Tears ran down Jade's cheeks as she turned away from me and sat down on the neighbor's sandy steps. She had rung the chirping doorbell several times. Thankfully, the neighbors had gone out, and no one answered the door. I sat down beside her and let her know that I would go wherever she went. I told her that I would never leave her. She climbed in my lap and cried. Then she said, "Grammy no go away."

I hugged her closely and rubbed her back gently, whispering in her ear, "I will never leave you." I also told her that she would get to go visit Grammy one day and that her brothers would miss her very much if she did not come home to see them.

Jade really struggled with good-byes. No matter how long she had known someone, she would get sad and angry whenever it came time to say good-bye. Her life had been full of good-byes, full of instability. To help her deal with the running away issue, I picked up a copy of the book *The Runaway Bunny* by Brown and Hurd. I wanted her to know that wherever she went, I would follow her (just like Momma Bunny) and bring her home.

In September she had a new teacher, a firm but kind teacher, who required Jade to participate in all the classroom activities. School meltdowns developed, the worst one being when Jade threw a chair, threw her shoes, and spat on the teacher. The teacher did not allow Jade to return to her classroom—ever. Thankfully, the director of the school allowed Jade to hang out in the nursery and help with the babies and toddlers, something she has always enjoyed. Her love for caring for small children likely began during her stay at the special needs orphanage, where she had the most mobility of all the children. After some time of observing Jade assist in the baby room, the director worked her back into one of the other kindergarten classrooms.

All summer long I had wondered if we had made the right decision for Jade. I knew she would not have much of a life at the special needs orphanage. I knew she needed a family, but could we be the family she needed? In October we took her to the doctor for a check-up. It had now been six months since we had brought Jade home. The doctor, a kind lady from India, read through the file that we had brought from the orphanage and then examined Jade. She remarked, "This is not the same child that is written about here. Whatever you are doing with her, keep doing it. You have done a wonderful thing for this child." We needed to hear those encouraging, affirming words.

When we adopted Jade at six years of age, she did not know her full name, she did not know colors, and she could not read or write in Thai. Physically, socially, emotionally and developmentally, she seemed more like a two or three year old. Cancer, chemotherapy and multiple hospitalizations greatly affected her development. Poor worker-to-child ratios also made it difficult for her to receive the input she needed to succeed educationally. Just six months after adopting her, Jade spoke and understood English, knew primary and secondary colors, enjoyed making new friends and blossomed in many ways.

Perhaps fireworks were not yet exploding in my mind. Maybe I could not yet hear the hallelujah chorus. A sparkler, however, glistened and glowed in the darkness, and I heard a faint rumble of hope building in the distance.

ALONG THE WAY
Step by step, He awards me faith for the journey.
Day by day, He meets my needs.
Week by week, He gives me the strength to carry on.
Year by year, He walks with me.
—Delana2000

11. Crawling and Walking

First you ARE mine; later you will FEEL like mine.
–Delana

One of the struggles we faced, not uncommon when adopting an older child, occurred on a weekly basis. Jade would hide items under her bed or pillow. Early on some of these items would be things she took without permission from her brothers, items like candy, gum and even money. After a while, she learned not to take things that did not belong to her. The desire to hide her own personal treasures under her pillow, however, has continued. Any money or special items she earns or receives often get buried in her bed. We think this stems back to orphanage days when "under her pillow" was the only private place for her. Although we would give Jade choices whenever possible, we also strove to help her understand the need to follow instructions and be a part of group activities. Our desire to do the best things for Jade did not always meet with what other parents thought best. In the first six months, several things happened that made being a good parent difficult. Some well-meaning friends thought we should have more "compassion" on her, bordering on pity, while we wanted to be consistent from the beginning on important issues like sharing, kindness, friendship, obedience and respect.

Once while attending a birthday party, the time came for all the girls to put away the toys and sit at the table for eating cake and honoring the birthday girl. Jade did not want to put away the toy she had and come to the table. A tantrum began. The mother of the birthday girl wanted me to give in to Jade by allowing her to stay by herself playing with the toy rather than requiring her to join the other girls in putting away toys and heading to the party table. I took Jade outside and gave her the choice of putting away the toy and joining the girls or going home right then. The easy thing would have been to let her stay by herself and play with the toy, but it would establish a precedent I did not wish to set.

Another time during the first six months, we went swimming at a friend's pool. Our friend's children were sharing various pool toys. After Jade had her ten minutes with a particular toy, she did not want to give it up for my friend's son to have his turn with it. My friend wanted me to give in to Jade and not require her to share it. She told her son to allow Jade to just keep playing with it, even though he and his siblings had been taking ten-minute turns with the treasured item. I said, "No, Jade also needs to learn to share." When I removed the toy from Jade and handed it to my friend's son, Jade began to throw a fit. She then had to spend time out of the pool. In her anger, she began to destroy her goggles, for which she promptly received discipline.

Friends and aunts and grandparents did not have to work with our child on a daily basis, and they were not given the responsibility to look down the road to what would be best in the long term. That job belonged to the parents. Unfortunately, early on it often meant that Jade decided she did not like me. Matter-of-fact, she would quite freely state that she hated me, that she wanted to move in with friends or grandparents, or that she wanted to return to Thailand. Though these times grieved me greatly (both her displeasure and the difference of opinions with my dear friends), I praised God for His strength to see me through.

In my experiences of raising three children, I knew about manipulation, testing boundaries and the need for tough love. I knew what she needed most desperately: consistency, routine, boundaries and unconditional love and affection (regardless of her attitude, disposition or obedience). I hoped that the bonding, attachment, expressed love and return affection would come with time; however, I determined, even when the affection was slow in coming, to be the mother she needed, the mother who would not reject her or abandon her or withhold the discipline when she needed it.

At this point, I did not yet feel like she belonged to me. I had prayed so long for a daughter to adopt. I waited until it seemed like she would never come into our lives. I expected to feel an instant connection with her, but that had not yet come. Interestingly, my husband bonded with her right away. We suspect that his bond came more quickly and naturally, because, for him receiving her into the family had similarities to each of the boys I birthed—the doctors handed each one of them to James and said, "Here is your child."

For me, I knew the deep emotions and attachment that came with carrying and bonding with an unborn child. When each of my sons came into the world, I already *knew* them in a way my husband could not. I remember James' awkwardness when he held our firstborn son. This time I experienced that awkwardness. I knew that this little girl belonged to me; however, I had to determine to love her even when that maternal bond had not yet developed. Anytime I would reach out to hold her hand (to cross the street or for a walk in the store) she would pull her hand away from mine and grab James' hand or the hand of another in our group. Sometimes she did this to James if he initiated the hand holding. If one of us made her mad by telling her she could not have something she wanted in the store, she would start removing or breaking items we had given her (shoes, bracelets, watches, necklaces, clothes, etc.). I decided that she could hate me, hurt me and horrify me, but I would choose to show love to her. I kept telling myself about Jade, "First you ARE mine, later I will FEEL like you are mine."

Would consistency in parenting pay off? Only time would tell. I certainly hoped it would. Jade began to learn that "Mommy means what she says," and challenges became less frequent; but they still remained part of everyday life. Bedtimes, shopping and sharing personal items were not the only areas that presented challenges. Even eating, which occurred at least three and sometimes four times a day, brought new struggles.

While learning about Jade's likes and dislikes, and while she adjusted to a new place, I tried to prepare familiar foods. If we were eating something totally new to her, her brothers and I would encourage her to try it, yet there were still plenty of healthful options on the table. Little by little she learned to like (or at least tolerate) foods that she had not been exposed to before. It did not take long for us to learn that sticky rice and fried noodles would be her all-time favorites and that potatoes (especially mashed) and all bread products would be her least favorites. Potato chips proved to be the exception. Chips, popcorn, and salty, non-healthy snack foods ranked high on her favorite foods list. Unlike many American children, however, she has always enjoyed raw vegetables like cucumbers, carrots and lettuce.

One day after she had begun to tolerate sandwiches (remember, she does not care for bread), I discovered that she would fill up on chips and refuse to eat anything else. Finally, on sandwich days I decided to place on her plate half of a sandwich, some raw veggies and a few chips. I would tell her that once she ate those items I would allow her to have a few more chips, if she was still hungry. She insisted that I put more chips on her plate "RIGHT NOW" before she had eaten anything. I refused, and a battle ensued. First she screamed and stamped her feet. I learned to laugh at her tantrums (since it eased my tension, not that it helped her, although occasionally it would diffuse her tension and make her laugh). When she noticed that the tantrum did not work, she fired away with manipulation tactic number two: "I not hungry. I not eat."

Hmmm. That was a new one. "Okay," I said, taking her plate and putting it out of reach. "Daddy and I are going to sit at the table and eat our lunch. Mommy will set the timer for five minutes. You will sit in this chair near the table and watch us eat. When the timer rings, Mommy will ask you again if you are hungry and want to eat." Five minutes later Jade decided that she would eat what I had offered her.

No problems occurred that day at dinner, so I thought she got the idea. I was wrong. By breakfast the next day she had already forgotten that this technique did not work. She wanted a larger bowl of cereal than I had given her. Leftover, soggy cereal is not good. So, I had started giving her small bowls of cereal, offering to give her more when she finished the first bowlful. "I want big bowl. Give me more," she demanded.

"Eat this bowl of cereal and Mommy will give you more."

"I not hungry," she declared. Pushing the bowl across the table, she stormed out of the room. I went after her and brought her back to the dining room to sit near the table while we ate our breakfast. Without saying a word to her,

I set the timer for five minutes. When the timer rang, she said, "I sorry. I hungry."

She had a desperate need to be in control. Her survivor skills and power plays kept her alive through abandonment, cancer, chemotherapy, pneumonia and moving around to different orphanages. We offered her choices whenever possible so that she could experience some control; however, many times if offered A or B she would choose C or say "no." She attempted to see who was in charge. Sometimes it felt like she was thinking, "If I'm in charge you cannot cause me trouble and make me sad, but I will become hard and block out the world. If you are in charge, I feel secure, but I will fight to be in charge because that is what I have learned to do."

Many times when told that she could not have a particular item, she would say, "I don't want it anyway," even if she greatly loved or needed that item. She seemed to believe that choosing not to want something hurt less than risking the disappointment of being denied. She became angry whenever visitors had to leave. Rather than see them off or say good-bye she would say, "I don't like them (or him or her)." Or she might say, "I didn't want them to stay anyway."

Think about it. If someone you have no feelings for whatsoever, says that they do not wish to be your friend, it does not bother you. But, if you had feelings for a particular person and then were rejected, it would hurt. So, for things to hurt less, Jade learned early on the art of choosing not to like or want certain things or people (even when she truly wanted or needed them).

As her new family, it became our responsibility to help her face her fears, desires and issues—such as abandonment— while teaching her love, trust, respect, forgiveness and hope.

The first time I realized one effect of abandonment was the time a friend came to visit us. Mary stayed for a couple of weeks and then had to return home. Jade became very angry and then sobbed uncontrollably. Jade struggled greatly with anyone coming into her life and then leaving. She could not understand short-term visitors. When any visitor would leave, in Jade's mind it was forever. In time, she would learn that James and I would not leave her; we were in this for the long haul. People could then come and go, but we would not leave. And she would learn of a Heavenly Father who rescues, comforts and loves her more than anyone on earth.

UNDER HIS WINGS

My God is like an eagle,
when I'm battered by the waves.
My God's like a snowy dove,
when I'm scared and afraid.
My God is like a mama hen,
when I've lost my way...
My God, He covers me.
My God is like a shield,
when the arrows fly.
My God is like a lighthouse,
when darkness fills the sky.
My God commands the angels
to lift me up on high.
My God, He rescues me.
My God, you comfort me.
My God, you rescue me.
My God, you love me.
(Based on Psalm 91 and Matthew 23).
--Delana2011

12. Forever Family

(He) adopted her into his family and raised her as his
own daughter. --Esther 2:7 NLT 2007

In one of my favorite bedtime stories to read to Jade, *Love You Forever* by Robert Munsch and Sheila McGraw, the mommy tells about her son growing up at various stages of life. Sneaking into his room at night, she would snuggle and rock him even when he reached his teenage years (of course he was sound asleep). While she rocked him, she repeated the refrain: "I love you forever, I like you for always. As long as I'm living, my baby you'll be." I wanted Jade to learn early on—and carry with her throughout life—that *forever* means until one of us dies. I wanted her to know that I would not abandon her.

In addition to the multiple books I bought and read to Jade about adoption (see appendix), I bought many books about family and read them to her nightly. Understanding what *forever* means was only part of the equation. She also needed to learn and experience what *family* means.

One day during first grade she came home in tears. Someone at school had evidently told her that I was not her "real" mommy. Though Jade had begun to speak English well, her understanding of English still trailed behind. This was normal, since cognitive development can take five to seven years. Explaining the concept of "real" mommy to an average first grader was difficult enough. How would I explain this to her? Using a variety of her adoption story books, we talked a lot that day about birth mommies

117

(tummy mommies) and how everyone has one. I told Jade, "Sometimes tummy mommies are not the ones to feed, dress, hug, kiss, and read to you and bandage your boo boos, so another mommy comes along to do those things. Some people have two mommies: a tummy mommy and a mommy who loves and takes care of them every day. Both are real mommies."

That day, Jade decided she wanted to write a letter to her tummy mommy. I told her that I did not have an address for her but that we could write the letters in a journal and save them for her. Every day that week, Jade dictated a letter for me to write in the journal for her tummy mommy. Most of the time it contained the same message: "Mommy, why did you leave me? I love you. I have a mom and a dad and three brothers and a dog. I am happy. I miss you. Love, Jade."

Some months passed with no desire from her to write letters to her birth mom. Other times, she had a need to do so daily. Some said I should not accommodate this desire. Others said that it was an integral part of her grieving and growing process. I tried not to make an issue of it either way, but made myself available to listen and aid her when she needed to express those thoughts.

When our daughter got mad at me or struggled with her adoption, she would tell me that she hated me, did not like me or wanted to go back to the orphanage. People who have never had children biologically would probably struggle more with this kind of rejection than I did. But, having raised three biological sons, I experienced times in their young lives where they would say, "I hate you!" So I could recognize the difference between a normal childhood expression of anger, when one does not get what one wants, and a personal attack.

From time to time, difficult heartfelt questions arose. My daughter wanted to know why her birth mother left her. Some parents have chosen to answer this by saying: "Your birth mom wanted to do what was best for you, and she could not take care of you." Of course, this might not be the full truth or even partial truth; the real reasons might not even be known. While I did not want to paint a horrid picture of her birth mother, I also did not wish to portray the event of abandoning one's child as "what was best." I did not want my daughter to wonder if one day I would become so poor or so sickly that I would then leave her for someone else to take care of her. I wanted her to know that I would be her *forever* mom, even in sickness, even if I became very poor. Only death would separate us.

I knew that her birth mother never got married. So I told my little girl that God's plan for families is for a man and woman to get married before they have children. I told her that her birth mom had not been following God's plan, which made it very difficult for her to take care of a family. I told her that when we stay close to God and follow His will for our lives He equips us to handle difficult situations including sickness, low income, etc. I hoped and prayed that as she grew up these things would reinforce in her a desire to stay close to God and a desire to wait to have children until after she married.

Sometimes Jade would ask me why I love her and why I chose her. She seemed to have an intense need to feel desired, to feel chosen. I told her how I had always wanted a little girl. I told her about the dream God had given me of adopting a little girl. I told her how we loved her best of all the children in Thailand who did not have a mommy and a daddy. In her first couple of years in our family, I also read to her the book *I'd Choose You* by John Trent. In this book, the author reinforces the concept of being chosen and special.

Once while at a friend's house, a boy Jade's age told me in front of her, in a very nanny-nanny-boo-boo kind of voice, *"I wasn't adopted. I have a mom and dad."*

I very quickly put him in his place and protected my daughter's heart by responding, "I am so sorry. Your parents had no choice; they just got stuck with you. We chose Jade to be our daughter." Perhaps that was a bit rough for him, but hopefully he discussed adoption with his parents and learned that it is not nice—or necessary—to tease a child for being adopted. Other times, Jade wanted to know why we did not adopt a sister for her. I simply told her that our house only needed one princess.

For couples desiring to start or expand their families, adoption can be a wonderful blessing. Although adopted children may grow to love their new families and be thankful for them, they have been dealt a very harsh blow in their young lives. Someone abandoned them. They carry a great weight of loss, pain and anger at a birth parent and/or God, and they may feel guilt and shame. Throughout their lives they will go through various grieving processes. While adoptive parents often celebrate "Gotcha Day"—the day they brought their child to live with them—holidays like birthdays and Mother's Day remind the child that they *Got Left.* Those days are often reminders to adopted children that somewhere in the world there is, or was, a woman and a man who look like they look but have decided not to be a part of their lives.

This creates the need for adopted children to go through the grieving process. And, this is why they must be shown that they have a heavenly Father who carries their broken hearts. They have a great big God who has a plan and purpose for their lives.

They need to regularly hear Jeremiah 29:11 (NIV)—

"For I know the plans I have for you," declares the LORD, "plans to prosper you and not to harm you, plans to give you hope and a future."

They also need to learn Deuteronomy 7:6 (NIV)—

"For you are a people holy to the LORD your God. The LORD your God has chosen you out of all the peoples on the face of the earth to be his people, his treasured possession."

HEART SLIVERS

I didn't break your heart,
someone else did.
But I know the One
who fixes broken hearts.
He gave me yours to hold.
I hold the pieces:
He's putting them together,
As I hold them in my hands.
One heart so tattered,
so many pieces, shattered…
Thump, thump, thump
Do you hear my heart?
It says…
I love you, I love you, I love you.
—Delana2011

Too often these days, the media reports that families return adopted children. This grieves me deeply. I have experienced the challenges of caring for an adopted child. I understand how easily, particularly in the first year, it would be for an adoptive family to want to give up. It took several years for our daughter to attach deeply to us and to develop vocabulary for expressing herself. Even though tantrums became farther and fewer between, occasional trying moments still arose. One day in her fourth year with us, I sent her teachers the following e-mail:

> *I am sorry that Jade missed school today. I gave her many chances and do-overs. Something was not right today. I could not even get her out the door without her kicking and screaming.*
>
> *The morning started out fine. She was excited while I began getting things out for beach day. She had a new way she wanted me to style her hair, and we had fun doing that and getting ready. Then it went downhill. I gave her choices and asked her about different things for her lunch. Then I added some apple slices to her bag, and she grabbed them and threw them out. She went from a sweet, happy little girl to a monster. It really did seem that way. In hindsight I wish I had stopped right then and prayed for her and me. I restrained my anger, trying to redirect her. She calmed down for just a bit.*
>
> *I asked her what she wanted for breakfast. "Nothing." I took out her medicine and vitamins and some of her favorite food. She threw the stuff off her plate. I should have disciplined her immediately at that point, maybe things would have improved if I had. I took a deep breath, held her face in my hands and looked at her eye to eye. I told her that I would give her another chance to be respectful and*

responsible. I warned her that she would not get her after school television privileges if she did not sit up nicely, eat something and take her medicine.

It was nearing time to leave, so I took her to the bathroom and asked her to wash her face and brush her teeth. She said, "I didn't eat yet."

I said: "You can take something in the car, but we will be late if we don't hurry."

She threw her toothbrush in the sink and began stomping her feet. Another fit arose—more massive than the others. She pulled the pony tails out of her hair, messing it up and screaming, "I don't want to go to beach day."

I tried really hard to make it a fun, light morning full of choices, mercy and grace. I did not want her to miss today. I wanted to just put her in the car kicking and screaming, knowing that she would likely be better for her teachers, rather than deal with what I knew would occur if I kept her home. I just didn't feel like it was the right thing to do.

At the point Jade realized she was not going to school, chaos ensued. She began destroying things in her room. I did not want her to break things or hurt herself, so I went and sat on the bed with her. She began screaming wildly. I wrapped her in a blanket, very tightly bound, and held her close. Many times she declared: I don't want you, don't hug me, don't touch me, go away, I don't want to be your daughter, you're not my mommy. I just held her tightly bound and whispered in her hair that I loved her, that I would always love her, that

I would never leave her, that even when she's mad at me I still love her.

She calmed down enough to beg me over and over to please take her to beach day. Amazingly, I stayed calm and droned on like a broken record every time she begged me to please take her. Finally, we went into the living room, and I held her on the floor cushions until she fell asleep, exhausted.

Please consider very carefully before entering the adoption process. Consider it a lifetime commitment, like marriage – Until death do us part. Realize there will be great challenges. Realize there will be deep needs. Understand that you will be tested by fire to see if you have genuine love. During the first year, I wondered if we had done the right thing for Jade by adopting her. During the second year, I knew we had done the right thing, but I wondered if I would have chosen to go through that experience again had I known what it would be like. In the fourth year, I reached a point where I would go through it all over again to have our precious daughter in our lives. When Jade first came to live with us, I had to choose to be loving and committed. Over time deep love—as deep as the love I had for any child I had given birth to—grew in my heart for Jade.

I do not remember the first time, but I have lost count of the times Jade has woken up in the night and sought me out. She needed me. She wanted *me.* She would tap me on the shoulder or stroke my arm and whisper in my ear, "Mommy, will you snuggle me?" At some point, she began to draw pictures for me; many of them were family pictures.

One day, Jade came home with a book she had made at school called "My Family." She made a page for each person in the family, drew a picture and wrote a sentence about what that person does. She said that dad makes great pizza. She said various things about each brother either being at college or studying Spanish. I really did not know what to expect when it came to my page. It could have been "Mommy spends lots of time on her computer." Or, "Mommy cooks a lot of food and washes our clothes." Instead, this precious daughter of mine wrote "Mommy likes to read books about Jesus."

We have observed another area in which Jade has grown tremendously—compassion. I told you how she showed compassion towards strangers who suffered from blindness, physical handicaps and illnesses. She also began to recognize children and adults who were sad, lonely, frustrated or discouraged, and she showed empathy.

Eventually, her compassion reached out and touched our family. Jade had never met my grandfather until the day before his death when she met him at the hospital. The very next day, upon hearing the news of his passing, she said, "Mama, let's take some roses to your grandmother." Even years after his death, Jade would tell me that she was sorry that my granddad had died.

Jade often would demonstrate her compassion and gift of mercy by making get-well cards and pictures for me or her father or brothers whenever one of us was sick. She would quickly shed tears when another person was sad or hurting. Teachers, other parents and friends began to recognize Jade's natural ability for being a leader. Her charismatic personality and her quickness in forgiving and forgetting a wrong done to her would draw people to her. When other children around her needed help, she would jump right in to help them out. Our daughter delights in bringing joy and creativity to the world around her.

When a child is born, a parent longs for the day the child begins to talk, particularly when the child first says, "I love you!" Somewhere along the journey, Jade began to say "I love you, Mommy!" And my heart melted. Often, she has expressed thanks for being adopted. Her laughter, giggles, teasing and joy have filled our home. Her brothers grew up and went off to college, emptying the nest. Thankfully, God had brought Jade into our lives before they left home. First, we chose her, and then she chose us.

A friend of mine also adopted an older child. Like me, she adopted a complete package—a child who already had likes and dislikes, a child who was the product of someone else's child-raising (or lack thereof) in the early formative years. Similar to our first few months and first year, she experienced great trials–more than once in a day—like the throwing of toys from the bed to the door at bedtime and meltdowns that occurred during meals or baths. Reflecting on the challenges of adopting an older child, I was reminded how much I have learned through adoption about God's great love for me and His love for the lost people around me who continue to reject Him. It reminded me of the price Jesus paid for me. I reflected on Jesus in the Garden of Gethsemane when the Bible says He sweat drops of blood while He was praying that this "cup" pass from Him—but that not His will, but God's be done.

The book of Hosea teaches us about a prophet who God tells to go and take a prostitute for a wife. He redeemed a prostitute, paid her debts, took her as a wife and showered her with love. She rejected him and returned to prostitution. God then told Hosea to go again and buy her back, which Hosea did for fifteen shekels of silver and some barley. Through this story God teaches us about His great love for His people. In Hosea 11, God tells us of all the things He did for the Israelites. He delivered them, held them in His arms, healed them, loved them, lifted their burdens and fed them. Yet they refused to return to Him. More than a story about a man and his wife, it was a picture of God's decision to choose a people and continue to love them regardless of their repeated rejection of Him.

I knew that just as God had told Hosea to go take Gomer as a wife, even though she would reject his love, God had clearly told me to adopt a child and love her as my own, despite her initial rejections of my love. He gave me nearly a decade of preparation; yet when the hour of trial began, I was not sure I was up for the task. I thought perhaps I had misunderstood God.

Adoption is a wonderful picture of God's great love for us. In the trials, the exhaustion, the rejection, we learn how to never give up, to keep on loving.

"Come, let us return to the LORD. For He has torn us, but He will heal us; He has wounded us, but He will bandage us" (Hosea 6:1 NASB).

Although the adoptive parent may feel wounded and need healing and bandaging, the more serious wounds are borne by the child. Our wounded princess, Jade, needed healing before she learned to return love and compassion. She began to show sincerity and repentance (something she could not do before). She began to see me not only as the one who said "no" and disciplined her for wrongdoing, but also as the one who would hold her when she was hurting, pray for her and with her, bandage her wounds and comfort her through nightmares. She also began to shower us with phrases we loved to hear:

"I love you! I'm glad you adopted me. I love my family. I'm glad you chose me. Sing to me about Jesus. Give me butterfly kisses. Pray with me. You're a good Mommy."

Through love, strength and guidance given to us from God, we daily saw Him transforming Jade into the beautiful princess that He created her to be. His perfect love truly cast out her fears (1 John 4:18). He gave her beauty for ashes (Isaiah 61:3).

Struggles became less, and she learned to truly be sorry for wrongdoing and seek forgiveness. In her first couple of years, the words "I'm sorry" often meant that she was sorry she was receiving discipline or sorry she was caught. One day during her fourth year, she had a meltdown and became angry and mean just before bedtime. I prayed with her before turning out her lights. She shook her head "no" throughout the prayer and voiced "no" several times. She resisted the prayer. No, she did not want forgiveness. No, she was not sorry. No, Jesus did not love her. I went downstairs exhausted emotionally and physically. I wondered if any of it would take root. I wondered how much was due to grief and bitterness and how much of it was a spiritual battle for her soul.

About twenty minutes after I had come downstairs, she came down and sought me out. "Mommy, I'm sorry for being mean. I love you!" She learned how to give and receive love; she had learned repentance.

Adoption is a commitment for a lifetime. It is a calling that is not for everyone; yet, it can be the most beautiful and most challenging thing you will ever experience. More than that, adoption gave us a precious, first-hand experience of God's love for us. Even while we opposed God and ran from God, He loved us. He cherished us. And, as His children, we know He will never leave us nor abandon us (Hebrews 13:5). First He loved us; then we loved Him (1 John 4:19).

A nine year pregnancy was our season of waiting on God, seeking Him, trusting that He would—in His time— answer our prayer. This season showed us God's faithfulness and guided us in believing God's nature. Perhaps you are waiting for God to answer your prayer for a child, for a mate, for healing or for direction. Remember that His nature is love, compassion, truth, strength. While you wait, hang on to Him!

THE CANYON

I am afraid of the canyons,
deep, dark wounds of the earth,
jagged edges, piercing, prodding,
slicing through the soft flesh,
ripping, tearing, burning . . .
I fear the making of the canyon.
But, then, comes the life-giving water
flowing through the crevice,
healing, soothing, nurturing,
providing beautiful flowers
and trailing vines, tall slender trees
to shade and cool,
creating a place of peace and hope
for its maker to rest His head.
--Delana2001

Appendix

Adoption books for Children—

God Found Us You (Harper Blessings) by Lisa Tawn Bergren and Laura J. Bryant

I Don't Have Your Eyes by Carrie A. Kitze

Over the Moon: An Adoption Tale by Karen Katz

Other helpful Children's books—

I'd Choose You by John Trent

Love You Forever by Robert Munsch and Sheila McGraw

The Runaway Bunny by Margaret Wise Brown and Clement Hurd

Adoption books for Adults—

Parenting Your Internationally Adopted Child: From Your First Hours Together Through the Teen Years by Patty Cogen

Twenty Things Adopted Kids Wish Their Adoptive Parents Knew by Sherrie Eldridge

Helpful Parenting books—

Boundaries with Kids: How Healthy Choices Grow Healthy Children by Henry Cloud and John Townsend

http://www.cloudtownsend.com/

Creative Correction by Lisa Whelchel

http://www.lisawhelchel.com/

Loving Your Child Too Much: Raise Your Kids Without Overindulging, Overprotecting or Overcontrolling by Tim Clinton and Gary Sibcy

http://www.timclinton.com/

http://mentalhealth.centrahealth.com/services/piedmont-psychiatric-center/itemlist/category/135

The Five Love Languages of Children by Gary Chapman

http://www.5lovelanguages.com/

The New Strong-Willed Child by James C. Dobson

http://myfamilytalk.com/

No More Meltdowns: Positive Strategies for Managing and Preventing Out-Of-Control Behavior by Jed Baker

http://www.jedbaker.com/books.htm

Parenting With Love and Logic (Updated and Expanded Edition) by Foster Cline and Jim Fay

http://www.loveandlogic.com/

When Love Is Not Enough: A Guide to Parenting Children with RAD by Nancy Thomas

http://www.attachment.org/

Made in the USA
Lexington, KY
13 October 2013